From Both Sides of the Desk

From Both Sides of the Desk
The Best Teacher I Never Had
by
Timothy Gangwer

Edited by C. David Keithley
Illustrations by Donna Kiddie

From Both Sides of the Desk

From Both Sides of the Desk
P.O. Box 691803
Houston, Tx. 77269-1803

-Edited and designed by C. David Keithley
-Cover Design and illustrations by Donna Kiddie
-Back cover illustration by Timothy Gangwer

ISBN 0–89896–338–9

First Printing – March, 1990

LARKSDALE

Printed in the United States of America

ACKNOWLEDGEMENTS

To my friends, colleagues, and teachers, who were once the seeds of yesterday's flower and have now blossomed into a wonderful bouquet of memories and experiences, your influence and support represent the binding of this book:

Bonnie Adams
Diane Albano
Alice Aull
Jaimie Ballingit
Nancy Bergmann
Mrs. Brauer
Kathleen Krainak Brooks
Toma Crandall
Mrs. Delahanty
Ellen Dempsey
Gloria Deveau
Jesse Ewing
Charles Feldhouse (Cubby)
Barrie Fleetwood
Maureen Harrington
Larry Imes
Donna Kiddie
Dan Kniola
Carl Kwiatkowski
Marie LaRocco

Dan Lutz
Kerri Lyons
Christa McAuliffe
Michelle Merrick
Ellen Meyers
Mrs. Milbranth
Lynn Dee Munson
Mary Ream
Rick Romano
Larry Sauer
Marcia Schiff
John Stark
Mrs. Tate
Robert Watson
Linda Wilke
Dr. Sylvia Williams
Steve Wilson
Todd Winski
Ken Zbell

Special thanks to John Schaefer for helping to make this book possible.

This book is dedicated to . . .

The adoring eyes of my parents
The companionship of my brothers
The love and support of my wife and children
The loving memory of John Owen Cook III . . . Johnny.

AUTHOR'S NOTE

From Both Sides of the Desk is the autobiographical account of the educational influences in my life as both a student and a teacher. As I adhered to a non-fictional format for this text, it was necessary to change the names of various individuals out of respect for their anonymity. Although I feel some will appreciate this alteration, I am certain others would be gratified to have it stand unchanged. To those individuals, I ask for your understanding.

-Timothy Gangwer

PROLOGUE

I often think back to when I was a child attending a county fair. I remember the bright lights and the dusty midway, the sticky cotton candy, exciting rides, and the call of the game masters beckoning my innocence. What I remember most is the chicken that played the piano. My excitement would build as I dug deep into my pocket for a shiny dime; then I would deposit the dime and wait for the show. The little stage lights would go on, the chicken would pluck out a quick tune for me, and the show would end. Now that I am older, I still retain those fond memories, but the story of the piano playing chicken has become symbolic to me. It is a story of dependence: My excitement depended on the availability of a dime. The stage lights depended on the deposited dime. The chicken depended on the stage lights. The piano depended on the chicken, and the food pellets that would drop into the feeding cup depended on the piano. It seemed pretty complicated just to give a farm animal a snack. It is, however, a pattern of learning and a method of teaching. Every element of the learning process depends on the effectiveness of what is taught. Therefore, teaching is a chain of events in our lives. I believe this chain may stretch, rust, or end, but it can never break. Teaching and learning are invincible forces – good or bad – and will remain so as long as there is life as we know it.

While writing this book, I was thrilled with the anticipation of its conclusion – being able to read it from cover to cover. When I finally had the opportunity, I laughed and cried. Watching a little boy treasure life's most precious gifts, only to have them torn away from him, and then his triumphant revenge in becoming a teacher, was an experience I wanted to share with both the young and the old. A child who loved to learn became an adult who loves to teach; this book is an attempt to capture the educational experience from both perspectives.

My purpose is to allow you, the reader, the opportunity to sit with me and swing your legs from a school desk once again, eventually becoming a mouse in the pocket of a teacher. These memories have given me a goal: to emulate the finest qualities in all of my teachers – to become the best teacher I never had. Anything less would surely be a disappointment to all teachers before me, as well as all those to come. For each experience shared, I hope to set the stage for a similar memory of yours: perhaps your first day of school, your first teacher, your first kiss, or maybe even your final day of school. Be it good or bad, uncommon or cliché, the goal of this book is to take you back for a moment in time: a time which has reserved a cherished moment for us all – a time when colors meant crayons, not ethnicity – a time of belonging – a time of friendship – a time to share the experience from both sides of the desk.

To live is to teach . . .
Being taught is life.

ELEMENTARY SCHOOL 1963

Hitchcock and *The Birds*
Medgar Ever's death
Sandy Koufax
The assassination of John F. Kennedy

KINDERGARTEN

My first recollections of school are of the year before I actually started. My brother David, who is seventeen months older than I, went to school one year before I did. Although kindergarten was only a half-day, his absence made it last forever. Not only was my lifetime playmate taken away, he was tasting the luxuries of independence without me. One might think that it would have been a golden opportunity to take advantage of some of the "only child" benefits, but I just could not bear the thought of what I was missing. On rainy days my mom and I would drive David to school. It was a huge brick building with stairs that took a great deal of energy to climb. At the top of the stairs were the magnificent doors that were four times the size of David. I remember pressing my face against the car window and looking through the raindrops as the huge building inhaled my brother. I worried about him at first, that is until he began bringing home his art projects and work samples. They were wonderfully colorful and probably some of the most incredible things I had ever seen. The next rainy day we drove David to school I noticed the stairs were much smaller and the building did not inhale him. In fact, he just walked right through the doors, which looked to be about twice his height.

That summer was definitely the longest summer of my life. It was hot, and there was absolutely nothing for me to do. I even had my lifetime playmate back, and yet I was bored. Thank goodness my birthday is during the summer. It proved to be a temporary diversion to my boredom — shadowed only by my anticipation of the beginning of school.

Finally the big day drew near. After what seemed like an eternity, my time to enter school had come. I will never forget hopping out of bed early to take my morning bath. Everything that day was new and unique. I scrubbed those thousands of little nubs on my head that my parents fondly referred to as a crewcut. I even took my hair crayon and waxed the top extra heavy that day. I can't really remember what I ate for breakfast; I guess maybe I was so excited that I forgot to eat. My clothes were new and stiff, and they made noise when I walked. They smelled just like the store we got them from, and we checked my shirt for stray pins. My shoes were so shiny I could see the clouds in the tops of them. The minutes seemed liked hours. I told my mom I would walk to school, but she said it was her job to take me on my first day, so I humored her.

When we finally arrived, the building had drastically changed over the summer. It had grown three times its normal size. It was breathing in and out, and children were running all over the playground screaming with terror. As the car door opened, David hardly said good-bye before being sucked out to the playground to join the others, frantically screaming and running for their lives. In a moment, he was gone. As mom turned the car off, I felt somewhat confused. She had just witnessed one of her children being torn from security, and I had the horrifying feeling that I was to be the next sacrificial lamb. I clung tightly to first the inside door handle and then the outside door handle. Finally, she suggested that we find, or rescue David. Then it happened. As we passed by the doors, which were now eight stories tall, the building took a ghastly surge of breath and sucked me in. It was so powerful, it even got my mom. The building was hungry that day. There were hoards of helpless children clinging to their mothers. Of course, my mom joined the other moms by hiding her fear behind an artificial smile. I remember some of the fibs my mom told me that day to alleviate my fears: "This is not its intestinal tract, it is a hallway; No sweetheart, this is not a gigantic stomach . . . it's your classroom."

That is when I saw her for the first time; she looked just like somebody's mom. She had a kind voice, and she crouched down low enough for me to see her eyes when she spoke. Her name was Mrs. Towers. I think she somehow knew I would grow up and write about her, so she was nice to me. Actually, the stomach of the building was not so bad after all. It had toys – more specifically, a large white airplane. The airplane and I became instant friends.

It all started to become quite pleasant, until I heard the most horrifying scream. It came from a large gray flying saucer mounted on the wall, or maybe it came from my mom. She had suddenly disappeared. She was gone–vanished into thin air. I never saw her again . . . until about lunchtime. It was not time to go home yet. Why did she have to come so early?

I guess it was because all of the other mothers were there. So once again I humored her and went home for the day. Mrs. Towers promised I could return.

As the days of kindergarten flew by, two peculiar things happened. First, the building stopped breathing and grew slightly smaller. Second, the white airplane became very difficult to claim. Looking back, I personally feel we could have used two of them.

FIRST GRADE

Cassius Clay
Vietnam
Three civil rights workers disappear
The Beatles come to America

Put simply, Mrs. Anders had a difficult act to follow. Not only was she lacking a white airplane, she had so many desks in her classroom that there was absolutely no room for our nap mats. Eventually, I agreed to trade mine for my very own desk. It was the type of desk that did not permit your feet to touch the floor. First grade was the year of the cigar box. My cigar box was smooth, clean, and new. Although it was exactly the same as everyone else's, it was much different— it was mine. It belonged to me, and the contents were priceless: round-nose scissors that gleamed in the light from the windows; stubborn crayons that refused to roll off the desk and proudly displayed their ephemeral paper wrappings; an eraser, which I kept immaculately clean (I suppose I made it a point to never make mistakes); and a pencil that was as red as a polished fire engine and as big around as two of my fingers taped together.

First grade was also the year of the Gonzalez twins. It is said that twins tend to think alike, and, of course, their parents dress them alike; that year, however, they aided me in a genetic discovery. Laughing uncontrollably, I discovered that the twins shared a lack of bladder control. I shouldn't have laughed, but I still find it humorous that Daphne and Christine wet their pants simultaneously. It was this observation that led to my first disciplinary trauma in school: no recess. I suspect Mrs. Anders found a private moment to appreciate the humor as well, but I doubt our custodian ever did.

I always wondered what went on while I was in the restroom. The restroom created a conflict for me. I noticed that most students would ask to "use" the restroom, whereas I chose to "visit" the restroom; it was an excursion. I figured it to be an even mile from the classroom door to the restroom door – quite a journey. I would pass a forest of brick pillars on one side and a collection of ordinal classroom doors on the other. Above me was a row of lights suspended from the ceiling by chains. They were white and had an intimidating hang to them. Their reflection on the perpetually shiny floor looked much like a sparkling bracelet. I liked to look at the reflection that the soles of my shoes set down as I walked. Once in the restroom, I would take permanent residence as an "independent" for one-hundred, eighty seconds, which was much longer than three minutes. Somehow hundreds of seconds seemed much longer than a mere few minutes. The restroom was all mine, that is, until another student came in or three minutes expired – whichever came first. The walk back was always quick, which was due, in part, to an empty bladder. As I reached for the door, I was reminded of what I had missed while on my adventure.

I learned that the fastest way to make a lot of friends is to split your head open on the playground. Thousands of small pebbles surrounded our blacktop, and as they were kicked, thrown, and blown onto the asphalt, they became the ideal assault weapon. This was the time Mrs. Towers reentered my life. It was she who peeled my lifeless body off the blacktop and sprinted toward the building. Crowds of concerned children trailed after her to see if the heroic casualty would make it until lunchtime. I remember my arms and legs flopping freely, resembling the jointless limbs of a much-too-loved Ragedy Andy. I worried about Mrs. Towers' expression of fear and my humiliation from flopping extremities. I displayed true grit while in the presence of the school nurse and never shed a single tear . . . until my mom came.

SECOND GRADE

**Sir Winston Churchill's funeral
Death of Malcolm X
KKK murder trial
Mickey Mantle**

Most of second grade was spent learning unusual things. Mrs. MacAllister spent an hour one day trying to convince our class that shaking whipping cream produces butter. This "farm knowledge" made me a bit skeptical, but my unrelenting doubt only accentuated the elation I felt when the magic lump began to bounce around the inside of my whipping cream carton. Butter . . . I made Butter! It was not just any butter, it was the best tasting, finest golden butter on the face of this earth. This butter was the product of my skepticism; even my mom pretended to like it.

The Jefferson Elementary School Annual Easter Fashion Show was to be presented by my class that year. I designed an Easter bonnet that compared to none. It was meticulously designed with a stovepipe motif, complemented by a bird's nest on top. After careful construction of my first endeavor in the competitive world of marketing, I was ready to model the latest in fashion for the parents: "Mr. Gangwer is seen here modeling his latest creation, 'Lincoln's Easter.' According to speculation, President Lincoln was pelted by a falling bird's nest while on a leisurely Easter stroll through the park with the First Lady. Due to the overwhelming height of his hat, the President never even realized the bird family had found a new home."

Just as Abraham Lincoln had given me art, the flutophone gave me music. Imagine seventy-five children sardined into

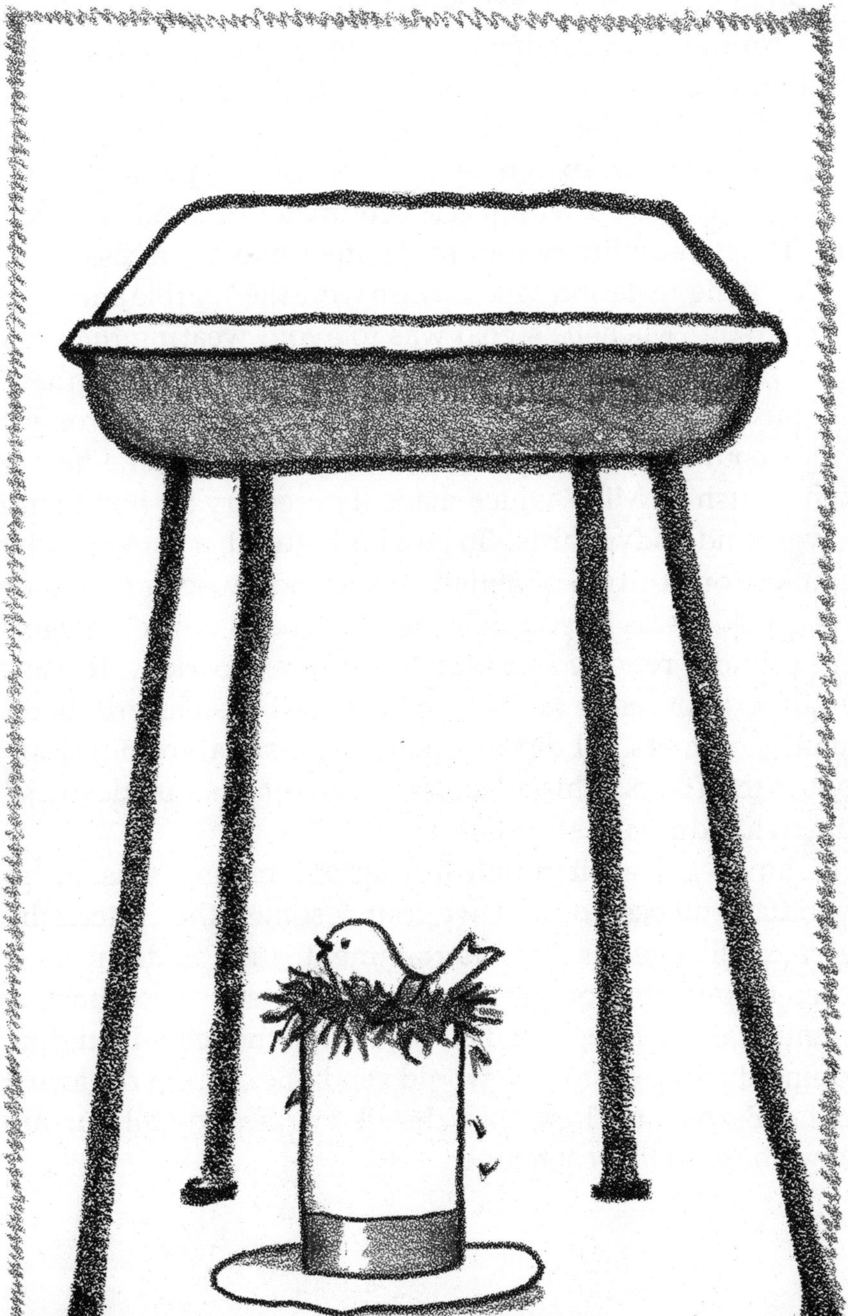

a small library with Mr. Taroady (a tall, skinny man with loose skin, ironically resembling that of a toad) playing our version of "Twinkle, Twinkle." It was not a pretty sight. The mouthpiece of the flutophone became a whistle when detached. In fact, it became an extremely loud whistle, especially when strategically placed within one centimeter of another child's ear. Thus, disciplinary trauma number two: no recess.

Michelle Teale and Mike Griffin were the "Barbie and Ken" of Jefferson. Michelle's goal was to avoid wearing the same outfit more than once in a school year. Mike had hair that, I assumed, was carved from wood. Not even the strongest winds could alter his "part of perfection." Michelle had an awful crush on Mike, which made it necessary for him to hire playground bodyguards. To be a bodyguard, a person had to manifest one of two qualities: broad and muscular, or short and quick. I was hired under the "short and quick" category and proudly reported for duty each recess period. It was a tough position, especially when Michelle began hiring "bodyguard slammers." I discovered that girls mature physically sooner than boys. This biological inconvenience made my job somewhat difficult at times.

Things got a bit rough during the mating season, but eventually it passed, and we found some other interesting recess challenge for our entertainment, such as daring each other to put our tongues on a frozen metal fence post, or intentionally kicking a ball on the roof of the school building, hoping that the custodian would send one of us to retrieve it. As for Barbie and Ken, they decided to destroy all our fun. They chose to like each other.

THIRD GRADE

Dangers of LSD
Discomania
Psychedelic art
Ducking the draft

Miss Milburn was my third grade teacher. She was indirectly responsible for my first kiss, or should I say my first sixteen kisses. I was hopelessly in love with Miss Milburn until she did the unspeakable – she got married. That left the second in line, Tammy Thomas, whom I cornered in the coatroom and kissed sixteen times on her left arm, while she hit me sixteen times with her right arm. Looking back, I think it may have been true love.

Milk time was 10:10 a.m. daily. We had wire milk crates, which were delivered to our door. The milk was ice cold and came in small glass bottles with paper lids. The straws were also paper and could bend like an elbow. I used to enjoy bending mine in several directions as I eagerly awaited my ice-cold milk. Although I enjoyed drinking it, my favorite part was the anticipation of being chosen to walk around with the crate and gather the empty bottles – a job worth killing for. 10:10 a.m. was a fantastic time of the day. I guess that is why I always felt so badly for the kids who did not pay their milk money. I tried not to look at their eyes.

I learned my first foreign language that year: French. I really enjoyed French, especially since it was probably the one thing I knew that my parents did not. I had a part in a play in which I had to ask the question, "Ou est votre livre bleu?" (where is your blue book?). Although I continued studying French through my high school years, today I only remember

one sentence: "Ou est votre livre bleu?" Maybe I was more interested in Miss Milburn than foreign languages.

Although it was a mere block, the honor and adventure of walking to school always promised daily action-packed experiences. I usually took my time so as to absorb any and all adventures that lurked between houses, on top of fences, under rocks, or in a classmate's pocket. Of course, there were those times when it became mandatory to sprint home. I can remember two in particular: when I exploded with excitement over a paper or project worthy of sharing, or when I had a recognizable wet spot in the front of my trousers. I often wondered when a child flew past me if they too were "drying the wet spot."

Mrs. Soetz was the famous Jefferson Elementary School Crossing Guard. She had blue hair and skin that shook when she yelled. Her uniform was dark blue and painfully stiff. Her stockings were a dull white, which allowed me the opportunity to marvel at her raised veins and peculiar bumps. Eventually my eyes would wander down to the surgical shoes, which always looked much too tight. She wore a hat similar to a policeman's hat. I recall being able to see myself in the black patent-leather bill as she bent down to reprimand me. Mrs. Soetz was kind, but stern. My mom said that was because she cared about me. I guess she used her authority as the weapon she needed to put herself between me and the things that were dangerous. I do not know if I ever thanked her for that. Maybe my eyes did that for me.

FOURTH GRADE

Three astronauts die in tragic fire
Newark riots
Detroit riots
Historic human heart transplant

I remember fourth grade as the "year of fear." I suppose Mrs. Ray was great to have as a neighbor; as a teacher, however, she had a wicked appearance. She had long, bony fingers and a voice that cackled when she spoke. She had peculiar spots on her arms; I assumed they were scars from the warts that had been removed. Although I never saw her broomstick, her classroom floor was always spotless, so I knew she had it stashed somewhere. Academically, I learned more from Mrs. Ray than any other elementary teacher. Looking back, I must confess she was an excellent teacher, full of enriching ideas and challenging lessons. I learned cursive writing that year, and if my penmanship was not absolutely flawless, it had to be redone. I felt important when I used a pen. They came in red and blue and put us back a whole nickel for each one. Everyone had the exact same pen, but mine was different. It was slightly bluer than everyone else's, and it was mine.

I acquired a deep respect for Elvis Presley's hit "All Shook Up" while in the fourth grade. Mrs. Ray believed that when your senses fell asleep, one only need to give them a good shaking to wake them up. For example, when I (accidentally) pulled the chair out from under Philip Gallaway as he tried to sit down, obviously my senses were sound asleep. Mrs. Ray was quick to wake them for me. She took hold of my shoulders and shook me until my eyeballs hurt from bouncing around in

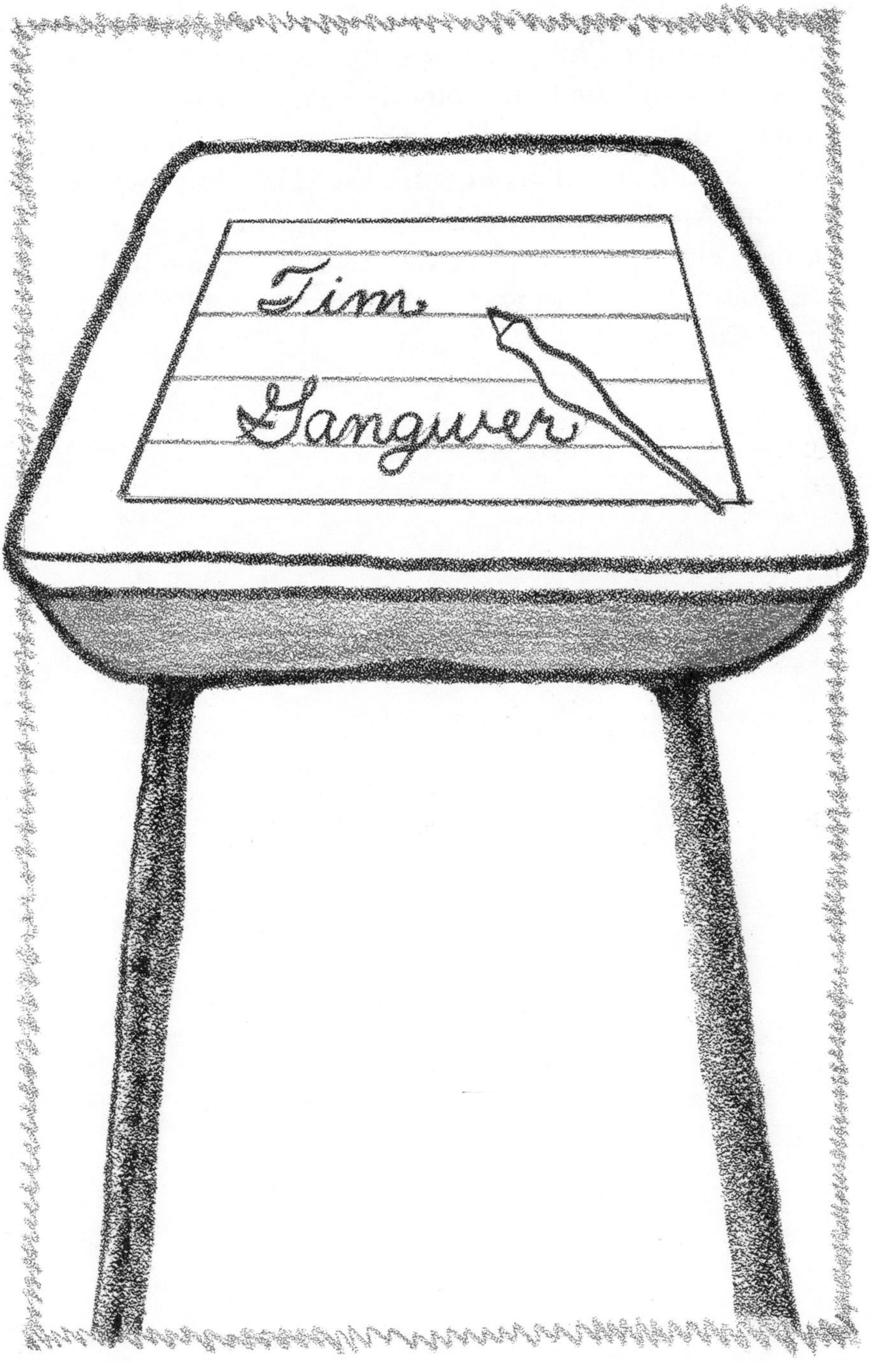
Tim
Gangwer

their sockets — thus, disciplinary trauma number three: no recess. Naturally, Philip hammed up his massive injuries, but he recovered in time to thoroughly enjoy recess.

Like it or not, square dancing was every Friday. I loved Ruth Richfield, and Sherry Lennis loved me, but I was forced to be Kay Appling's dance partner. Kay was approximately nine feet, eight inches tall. I was two feet, three inches tall. Need I say more. Ruth was every bit as tall as Kay, but then, love is blind.

FIFTH GRADE

Assassination of Martin Luther King
Assassination of Robert Kennedy
Jimi Hendrix
The Nixon era begins

At the time, I did not realize fourth grade was to be my last year at Jefferson Elementary. I was torn between feelings of excitement, sadness, anticipation, and fear. My family moved just prior to fifth grade. Although I had mixed emotions, I have always enjoyed change. I knew I was in for a real adventure when I heard the name of my new school coupled with the principal's name: Joy Elementary School — Leo Crabbs, Principal.

Deep down I hoped my new teacher would look like somebody's mom. I hoped that she would crouch down low enough to see my eyes when I spoke. Mrs. Delaney never had the opportunity to know how much I liked her; I was too busy using her as my punching bag so the other students would accept me. This was to be the year I learned a new word: "surly." Not only did I learn its meaning, I also learned what it looked like printed in red ink on the back of a report card. Even worse, I learned what it felt like to receive a negative comment from a teacher.

Since I was buck-toothed, I was quickly labeled "Buck." I accepted this as a way to be recognized regardless of its negative connotation. After a few weeks, the time had come. I knew something had to be done. There were no pebbles on the blacktop, so I couldn't fall and crack my head open again. Therefore, I chose instead to dislocate my finger during a playground softball game. Although this was not my first choice of solutions to the problem, it had the same "pebbles on the blacktop" effect. There were, of course, a few differences. For example, Mrs. Towers was unavailable, but I noticed the crowds of concerned children trailing after me. The following day I was issued a finger splint and a new identity: "Tim."

Actually, it proved to be a fairly productive year. I switched from flutophone to the coronet, played Beatles' songs on the autoharp ("Twinkle, Twinkle" had lost its pizzazz), drew detailed pictures of Abraham Lincoln, received my first "D" on a report card, and heard *Charlotte's Web* for the first time.

One of the most tension-filled periods of the fifth grade was from February tenth to the fourteenth. On the tenth, our class designed valentine bags and hung them in a row with the understanding that we could bring our valentines to drop in the bags at our leisure. During that incredibly long four-day period, anytime I was out of my seat I made it a point to take an inconspicuous stroll down "Valentine Bag Lane." The tension would build as I passed each bag, wondering if mine would be as full as the others. Popularity was not based on personality, achievement, or athletic ability; it was based on the number of valentines in your bag. Mine was full by the fourteenth, but I must confess . . . I gave myself a valentine that year.

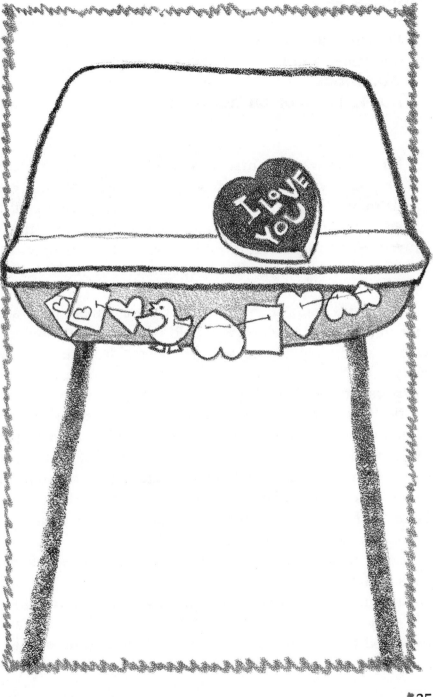

SIXTH GRADE

Woody Allen
Education crisis
Woodstock
Apollo 11 – Man on the moon

Mr. Davis was my first male teacher. He was a short, balding man with a pudgy physique. He had the ability to juggle many subjects, which was a necessity since my class included both fifth and sixth grade. This combination actually proved to be an academic incentive for me. I was determined to ensure that none of the fifth graders were in a higher group than I.

Mr. Davis had a unique behavior management program, known as "Court," which was held every Friday. Students were tried and sentenced by their peers. If a student was placed on "the list" at any time during the week, they had to appear in court that Friday. I may have regarded this as a dictatorial system of classroom management had it not been for the occasional humor involved. As an eleven-year-old, I wonder if I began equating inappropriate behavior with crime. The various punishments included such things as eating lunch at the girls' table or singing "Mary Had a Little Lamb" in front of the entire class. I had a lot of fun with court – that is, when I was one of the jurors.

I got braces on my teeth that year, was pelted with snowballs for falling in love with Carolyn Simmons, and was constantly in trouble for having my shirt tail untucked. I did not get the part I wanted in the play, and Mr. Davis rarely passed the ball to me during recess football games. Also,

during the winter we had to leave our snow boots outside the classroom door in the hallway. Inevitably, my boots would always generate the largest puddle. I enjoyed being a safety patrol and one of the first-string halfbacks on the Joy Elementary School Flag Football Team. I remember being angry a lot, especially the time Mr. Davis made Leanne Downing cry with his unwarranted sarcasm as she struggled to use the shadowscope. I felt bad for her. I tried to look at her eyes; somehow I knew that my eyes were the perfect match for hers.

Perhaps I learned more in sixth grade than any other grade, but I really didn't care for most of what I learned. I decided that year I wanted to become an aviation flight technologist. I didn't know what an aviation flight technologist was or did, but it sounded important, and I wanted to be important – unlike the image I had of my teacher.

JUNIOR HIGH SCHOOL 1970

Robert Redford
Population concerns
Kent State Killings

SEVENTH GRADE

I wore my favorite shirt on my first day in seventh grade. It was an American flag shirt. I cannot remember if it was my favorite shirt because Abbie Hoffman wore one, or because I was born on the Fourth of July. Maybe both reasons – maybe neither, but I did manage to wear it for my school picture that year. I lived on the outskirts of town and was bused to Elston Junior High School. Since it was a predominately black, inner-city school, they needed me to help tip the racial scales. That was the first year I had ever ridden a school bus. From the very first day of school, I always made it a point to sit in the back of the bus. That way I could observe what everyone else did once they boarded. Also, once we arrived at school I had the opportunity to assess the social situation while everyone else got off. This assessment period proved to be quite valuable in the days to come.

In our school library, there was a long metal tube that snaked its way down from the second floor to the ground. It was an emergency fire slide, but I felt compelled not to wait for an emergency. I was intrigued with the amusing potential it had hidden inside its dark, twisting belly. Approximately one week into the school year, I noticed a frantic crowd forming at the bottom of the emergency fire slide. Due to my small physique, I managed to squeeze my way through the tangled maze of students, only to find a classmate having a severe epileptic seizure. Since I had no experience or knowledge of such a disorder, I remember thinking it had been a result of using the emergency slide in the absence of an emergency. I spent three years at Elston and never once used the slide. In fact, I avoided it.

I loved the first few months of junior high. The change was nice, I made loads of new friends, and I had my own home, which some students referred to as a "locker." Although all of the lockers were identical, my locker was cleaner, brighter and tidier than the others . . . it was mine. I also had fabulous teachers, but best of all, I sat directly in front of Pam Kaplan. Pam had developed physically at an age when young boys, especially me, might appreciate her. Why was my seat location so important? Pam would taunt me into turning around at least six times during class. Each time, two things would happen – (1) the teacher would have her back to the class, and (2) Pam would release a button on her blouse (there were usually six). Core curriculum was tough in seventh grade, but I did master the skill of discriminating left from right, right from left, and all points between. I probably would have learned a great deal more had Pam taught the class . . . a great deal more.

I was told I was too small for football, so I went out for the track team. I took it very seriously because I had a great admiration for my dad. He was a hurdler – an incredible hurdler. In his prime, he could out-hurdle any of his competitors; he could out-hurdle the best. I very much wanted to be the hurdler my dad was. Although he gave me many good qualities, hurdling was not one of them. I felt I owed my dad when it came to being a hurdler. On my fourth birthday, my family had a get-together with several friends and relatives. I remember begging my dad to hurdle our picket fence for everyone. Eventually he consented. His clearance, however, was a little short, and he hurt himself very badly. I remember wanting to take his place, but I was too little. Perhaps I carried the guilt into seventh grade as I once again tried to take his place and, once again, could not.

It was 1971, and by spring I had made lots of friends. Some were black and some were white, but I don't remember caring about such insignificant things as race or skin color. Two weeks into the spring, I belonged to Section 7-3. This meant the third group of white students in grade seven. We were escorted to each class by armed Indiana National Guardsmen to ensure our physical safety. Why did my black friends suddenly hate me because I was white? I did not know, but I desperately wanted to know. I do not remember what was more intimidating – the look on the guardsmen's faces or the rifles they carried. I saw interracial extortion (sometimes I would have to go a week without lunch due to the dreaded phrase, "Gimme a dime man!") I saw my teachers violently beaten in the hallways. I saw chains on the doors so that the white students would not flee the building every time news of violence broke out. I saw black arm bands; I saw white arm bands. I saw clenched fists, angered faces, weapons, and threats. The worst thing I saw was something in myself: fear.

I cut my hand in art class with an X-acto knife, which resulted in three stitches. I had no idea at the time it would be a similar knife that would cut me again, only this time as a result of racial tension.

Physical education class was in a separate building. On this particular day I was late and therefore separate from Section 7-3. While traveling between buildings, I was taken by surprise and beaten by four black students. The confrontation intensified when I was physically pinned against a brick wall by three of the students. The fourth student was carrying an X-acto knife and wearing an angry grimace. As he approached me, I remember worrying I would have to get more stitches. He said many things, none of which I heard. Perhaps it was the sound of my own heart beating in my head that stifled the sound of his voice. I did not think he would cut me. After all, we knew one another as classmates. I yelled in horror, "Stop! Don't!" I failed to finish the word "don't" before he responded with, "Shut up!" With each syllable he spoke, he thrashed the blade down the center of my tongue. There was a lot of blood. Then my attackers absorbed my fear and left me on the ground next to the knife. The pavement felt cold against my cheek. I watched their tennis shoes scramble in a confused pattern before disappearing completely. I cried for what seemed like a very long time. I remember vomiting from a combination of terror and swallowing too much of my own blood. I threw away the knife and went to clean up. No one saw me. I cried at the sight of myself in the restroom mirror, and the fear quickly returned. I was pale and scared. My trembling hands fumbled nervously with the paper towels as I tried to doctor myself enough to cover the trauma. My tongue had swelled enough to make it feel as though I had a mouthful of food. I wanted to hide in the restroom until this part of my life passed.

By this time my bus had arrived, and I was drawn to its security. I remember sitting in the front seat; I no longer had a reason to go to the back. I had a good assessment of the social scene.

I always thought it was strange that no one ever questioned my whereabouts during physical education and I was counted as being present. My parents never knew of the incident. As difficult as it was, I knew my mom and dad would deal with it in such a way that would endanger me again. I felt sorry for myself because I never gave anyone else the opportunity. If my memory serves me correctly, I ate soup quite a bit. With the exception of the final few weeks of school, the violence and consequential escorting continued. Thereafter, at the first sign of violence, I left the building. I never went to physical education alone again. The student who cut me was named James Harper. Over the years we were on speaking terms except, of course, during each spring. My tongue never adequately healed, nor did my feelings. Although I did not tell my parents, I am sure they would have discouraged any bitterness with comments like, "You were cut by a student, not an ethnic group." As for James Harper . . . I never looked at his eyes. I guess he never really gave me the chance.

EIGHTH GRADE

High school pregnancy
Jane Fonda - relentless activist
Jesus Christ Superstar
Disney World opens

The key to emotional stability for an eighth grader is having the ability to catch the eye of one of the school cheerleaders. Not only did that make me emotionally stable, it created self-esteem that mitered into a wonderful frame of mind. Her name was Linda Wilkinson. She had blond hair, blue eyes, my height, and best of all, she had something in common with my mom: she loved me. She also had a couple of things in common with Pam Kaplan. Since Linda was a cheerleader, I instantly took a great interest in basketball. One time I even watched a game. Linda did not give me self-esteem, but she did remind me that I possessed it. Even when she moved to another city, I remained the person I was before she left. I fondly remember her for that.

English was not a class, it was an experience. Two eighth grade classes were combined into a team-teaching setup starring Miss Templeton and Miss Perkins. I have vivid memories of each teacher; they were both extremely large women. To this day, every time I hear the sound of material rubbing together, I think of one of them coming down the hallway. I read Romeo and Juliet for the first time that year. I remember wondering, "Why do we have to read this junk? Nobody talks like this anyway."

Since I spoke of my favorite shirt, I suppose it is only fair to give my favorite pants equal billing. They were blue, bell-bottom hiphuggers with bells so large I could no longer see the

clouds in the tops of my shoes. Hiphuggers made me feel like I always needed to pull up my pants. I guess I felt "cool" as we used to say, or perhaps "hip." I liked them so much that when I outgrew them, my mom sewed a strip of material on the bottom of each pant leg to compensate for the length. The material was white with a continuous row of navy-blue peace symbols all the way around. Maybe I should have worn the pants more often during the spring months. After all, since everyone seemed to be looking down at one another, maybe someone might have noticed my pant-length message.

The racial rioting continued that year, and I learned to keep a low profile. Also, the local fire marshal slapped a few administrative hands for chaining the doors, so I frequently left when the violence erupted. I do not really remember as much rioting that year as in the previous year. Maybe there was the same amount, but since my status changed from "student" to "war veteran," I didn't notice it as much. I guess it's safe to say that by eighth grade, I had been in the trenches.

NINTH GRADE

Governor Wallace shooting
Mick Jagger
Murders at Munich
Harry S. Truman dies

Ken Nelson was his name. He took an interest in what I had to say and the way I did things, even though my way may not have been typical of most ninth graders. For example, I remember an important research assignment that had to be presented as an oral report. The thought of it bored me to the point of being ready to settle for an average grade. Sensing my attitude, Mr. Nelson encouraged me to do something that was important to me, "like music." Don McLean had a hit song on the radio entitled "American Pie." I decided to analyze the lyrics of the song, verse by verse, for my presentation. I felt good about a conversation I overheard in the hallway between Mr. Nelson and another teacher concerning the quality of my report. From that day on, I appreciated anything Mr. Nelson had to say.

This was to be the final year before entering that social celebration of academics, commonly known as "high school." As a ninth grader, my intentions were to grab the udders of experience and milk the many advantages of being "King of the Hill" with the gratifying knowledge that all of the other students in the school were younger and not nearly as wise. I did not need the assistance of a cheerleader any longer. I even got the braces off my teeth that year. Between seventh and ninth grade, I grew three feet taller, yet my measurable height remained the same.

Today, Elston Junior High School no longer exists as I knew it; the city thought it was a great place for a parking lot. As the walls crumbled under the destructive arm of modern renovation, I hope the anger and tension absorbed in each brick crumbled with it. I often think about the pigeons that attended Elston in 1971. Spikes and nails were defensively placed in their living quarters, so they could no longer come and go as they pleased. It seemed their presence was defacing the cosmetic value of the building, and they were therefore driven away from something I am sure they thought they wanted. They too were subjected to the chained doors of the times. Today, the pigeons and I need only to reflect on what was a critical and often cruel chapter in the lives of many to understand the importance of unity, fairness, and caring. The Elston Junior High School of yesterday is now the parking lot of today. 1971 is forever ground into the asphalt, so today's children can put themselves above it and maintain the school experiences they deserve. As for the pigeons, I have decided to believe that someone created a wonderful, comfortable home for them – perhaps that "someone" was Mrs. Towers.

SENIOR HIGH SCHOOL 1973

Thomas Bradley becomes Los Angeles mayor
Vice President Spiro T. Agnew resigns
Gerald R. Ford becomes the 40th Vice President

TENTH GRADE

With junior high behind me, it was time to step into a new arena. Rogers Senior High School was located in the country, not far from my home. The school was fairly new and had been built on farmland, more commonly known as "mud." Surrounded by cornfields, it was the perfect educational hideaway. It was amazingly large, and the halls were long and wide. I remember how the masses of students would emerge from the classrooms at the sound of the bell, resembling the chaotic scramble of a busy ant hill.

Tenth grade was the "year of the ear." I discovered I had a very perceptive ear for music. During my Music Theory class, I was able to identify various intervals on the piano with 100% accuracy by ear alone. I thought I had found something

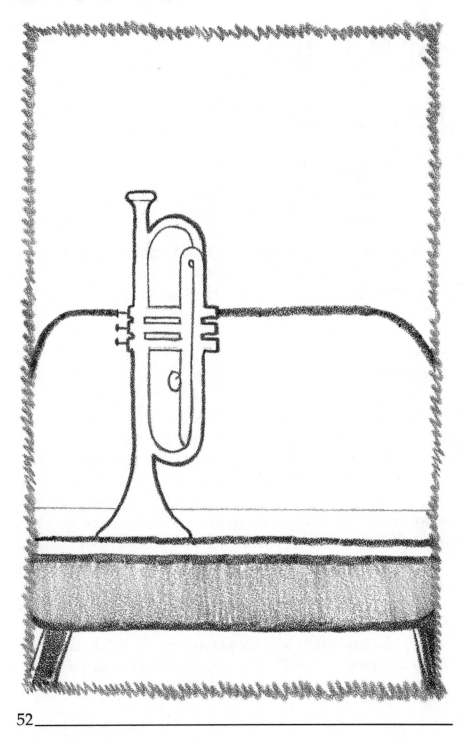

I was not looking for. My talent seated me in the trumpet section of the high school band. I thoroughly enjoyed the activity of the band, as opposed to the "listen and learn" concept emphasized in other classes. It was very gratifying to be rewarded by a teacher for intentionally creating consistent classroom noise.

Mr. Johnson was the theater/drama teacher. He was a nervous man with thinning hair. He had five pairs of polyester slacks, varying only in color, which he rotated accordingly throughout the week. Due to the stretchable nature of his pockets and the fidgeting mannerisms of his personality, Mr. Johnson seemed to spend every possible moment fumbling with his pocket playground equipment. His favorite toy was a disposable lighter, which he would frantically flick without activating the flame. It was only a matter of time before he reduced his polyester slacks collection to four pairs. As my class began to chuckle at the smell of his singed leg hair, his pocket flashed into a puff of smoke. As a teenager, I gained an instant respect for the dangers of smoking. We had a substitute teacher for the next three weeks. I guess one could say Mr. Johnson was experiencing the frustrations of "burn-out."

ELEVENTH GRADE

Patricia Hearst kidnapping
Watergate
Hank Aaron breaks Babe Ruth's record
Nixon resigns

Mrs. Lark was my creative writing teacher. She had a distinct nasality in her voice, which was far too articulate. She caught my attention with the announcement of a contest. Anyone could win by having their creative efforts published in the school newspaper. My poem was entitled, "The Transaction of Mankind." I was excited. I had produced a poem packed with colorful, three and four syllable words that rhymed with a flowing elegance of sincerity. Although I did not understand most of the words, I used them to impress myself and tease my potential. Through my excitement, I wondered if I had found a new talent. I almost phoned Mrs. Lark at home during the weekend to give her a personal recitation.

We submitted our creative masterpieces on Monday and eagerly awaited Tuesday's publication announcements. The following day, Mrs. Lark boasted that twenty-five of her twenty-eight students had made the newspaper. I sat so proudly with anticipation that my back never touched the seat. As she finished enthusiastically announcing the "talented winners," she concluded by returning the rejects with a condemning tone: "Unfortunately some people in this room feel big words make a poem. This misconception has excluded some people from the school newspaper. Perhaps if some people paid attention in class a little more, they would not only understand the words they choose, but also how to use them." With each word she moved closer to my desk. The final words

of her sermon were accompanied by the return of my attempt at creativity, which had now turned to humiliation. I remember wishing I had phoned her over the weekend and therefore avoided her disheartening critique in front of my classmates.

I wore three-inch platform, blue and burgundy suede shoes that year and drove a 1946 Pontiac to school each day. I quit the band and joined the rock group "Halic," shattered my front teeth in an automobile accident, let my hair grow to my shoulders and wrote a term paper on exorcism for my Health and Safety class. The approaching summer vacation was perhaps the most gratifying element of eleventh grade. At the close of the school year, I knew it was time to corral some of my energy into something of significance — like part-time employment.

TWELFTH GRADE

**Hoffa is missing
Twelve-state teacher strike
The Godfather and *Jaws*
The ozone layer**

I was employed by a major shoe chain located in a large shopping mall in Michigan City, Indiana. Ultimately this position became the motivational strength behind my decision to go to college. Evidently, I was a natural with people, and I developed a fine-tuned ability to say things people wanted to hear. I should have recognized this ability as the first step to a political career. Needless to say, my talent was applied to selling snow boots in the heat of summer, sandals in the chill of winter, purses to men, and polish for suede shoes, all with a dangerous degree of sincerity.

As time passed, retail divorced education. Education was forced to take a backseat. Grades went down while sales went up. Once again it became necessary to humor my mom by agreeing to take the famous college entrance exam: the Scholastic Aptitude Test (SAT). Due to my mom's consuming hours of hopeful diligence, I even went as far as to sign the college application she had filled out.

After one year of sales stardom, I was offered a slot in the Manager-in-Training Program to immediately follow my long-awaited high school graduation. It was tempting, as it offered success, money, and power. It really seemed like the American thing to do, but it came time to humor mom again. A visit to Ball State University in Muncie, Indiana was all she asked. How could I refuse. After all, it only required two days away from the retail playground and even David Letterman went to good ol' "Ball U."! Maybe I felt I had not given education a fair shake throughout the high school years. Maybe I felt I owed it to my mom's caring persistence. Maybe I felt I owed it to myself.

On a scale of one through ten reasons, I gave the overall college visit a solid seven: (1) It was alive with people; (2) The people all looked like me; (3) It was absolutely unique and novel; (4) The people all looked like me; (5) I felt a strong sense of independence and a sense of belonging; (6) The people all looked like me; and (7) My parents and I watched each other with adoring eyes. Regardless of the outcome, the pivotal issues in my life – education, lack of education, and destiny – all became quite real. It actually scared me. I really do not remember what scared me more – the decision between education as opposed to success, money, and power, or the absence of the adoring eyes that watched me become what I was, and was not.

Since I gave college a solid seven on my rating scale, the remaining three points were awarded to retail: (1) Success; (2) Money; and (3) Power. I took a long, hard look at myself and realized that none of the people in the Manager-in-Training Program looked like me. I had frightening images of myself trapped in my hometown, surrounded by the smell of leather for the remainder of my life. I no longer felt the unrelenting desire to humor my mom. It didn't matter that David Letterman went to Ball State University. It didn't even matter that I was going to be absent from the retail playground. What did matter was the effectiveness of my rating system. Therefore, it was clear that I had to reevaluate. For the first time in many years, I invited education into my life, as opposed to avoiding it. I was going to college.

Graduation night arrived. As the proud parents – equipped

with tissues and cameras – packed the gymnasium, I began scanning the many rows of my fellow graduates. I realized we all looked the same. We no longer paraded our personas with the ornamental prestige of athletic letter jackets, cheerleading outfits, concert T-shirts, and monogram sweaters. We were disguised in generic, light blue robes, which created a welcome air of equality. Regardless of our popularity status, athletic ability, and academic achievements, we all ended up in the same place having the same appearance, but we would all be going in different directions once the robes were removed.

As the excitement and anticipation of walking across the "stage of accomplishment" began to build, I felt important. I remember squeezing the congratulating hand of Mr. Williams with one hand, while squeezing the cover to my diploma with the other. The cover was a magnificent, blue vinyl embossed with metallic gold lettering. I waited until I reached my seat to enjoy its long awaited contents. Much to my surprise, it was empty with the exception of a small, standard note: "Due to an untimely printing error, all diplomas will be received by mail at a later date." It was the closing curtain of a play with poor reviews.

As I lump my memories of high school together, I find my recollections to be somewhat brief, but it was definitely one of the longest periods of my education. There are many times when I think that those years represented my childhood occupation, and yet, they probably did not. An occupation becomes a matter of individual choice. For example, if one chooses to terminate an occupation at any given time, it is only a matter of doing so. Although there may have been several times I deemed it necessary, somehow I am not convinced that my parents would have agreed with my attraction to taking a

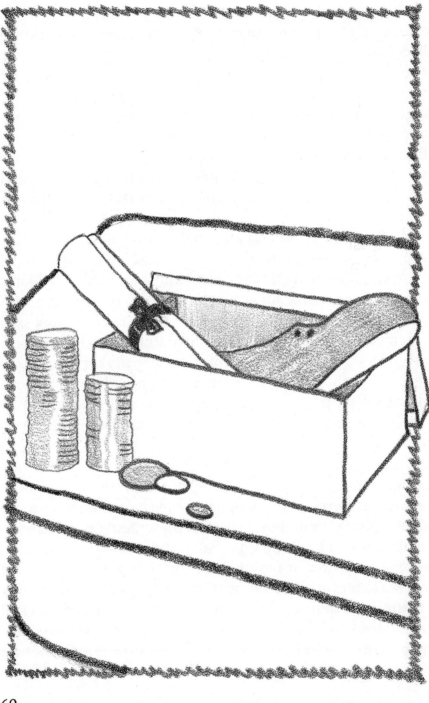

few years off from education. In fact, I am positive that the Indiana State Education Agency would have enlarged their fine print in protest of my decision.

High school pilfered my childhood innocence. Although I felt the presence of my childhood, it was always one social step from my reach. It seems education had become nothing more than a reason to put lots of people of the same age group in one building. Most of my teachers inadvertently provided me with valid reasons not to become an adult, except Mr. Williams. It was his bushy-eyebrowed assertiveness that diverted my perception of education. He taught me several things, most of which I never learned, but I did learn something that would eventually prove to be an enormous stepping stone in my life and career. I learned what a teacher is. I had already learned what a teacher is not, and I remember thinking that Mr. Williams did not fit that mold. Actually, that in itself captured my classroom attention. His formula was simple. He was one part Horace Mann and one part Johnny Carson. He did not talk at me, he talked with me. He did not say things he thought I wanted to hear, he said things he wanted to say. He was not as concerned about *what* I learned as he was concerned *that* I learned. I remember wanting to absorb some of Mr. Williams' personality and educational philosophy. I think maybe I did.

COLLEGE
1976

One Flew Over the Cuckoo's Nest
James Earl Carter wins presidential election
Viking 1 & 2 land on Mars
Chicago's Mayor Richard J. Daley dies
Educational mainstreaming
Annie Hall
Pope John Paul I dies
Guyana tragedy
Three Mile Island accident
Jane M. Byrne is elected mayor of Chicago
Deer Hunter
**Margaret Thatcher becomes Prime Minister of
  Great Britain**
Mount St. Helens erupts
53 hostages in Teheran
U.S. boycott of the Moscow Olympics
Who shot J.R.?

Although I figured out what an aviation flight technologist was, I no longer had the desire to become one. I was admitted to Ball State, providing that I participate in the Academic Opportunity Program, which was the university's way of telling me I had poor SAT scores. At first, the pressure of the program became a sink or swim situation. As the introductory days passed, it became apparent that the first block of required courses were quite simplistic and geared toward keeping me in school.

The time had come to evaluate the educational system once again and to decide what my role was as a college student. A college student had to have a strong sense of responsibility and self-discipline. A college student needed to exercise a financial budget conducive to the purchasing of textbooks and supplies. Finally, a college student had to have a hunger for knowledge and a thirst for success. I, however, had a large appetite for pizza during the day and an overwhelming thirst for beer at night – especially on Friday and Saturday. Since some of the textbook prices cut far too deeply into my budgeting strategies, I was forced to read assignments and study for exams while sitting cross-legged in the aisles of the student bookstore. After all, how else does one purchase the mandatory amount of pizza and beer with that consistent nag otherwise known as "the book price stigma"? Of course, the responsibility element I referred to was mostly present on the weekends. I was responsible for my thirst, as well as my coherency the following morning.

Whether or not I fit the mold, life as an "average" student was good, but I must not have had the appearance of an average student. While sharing an elevator with two professors in the teachers' college, I listened to their exchange of frustrations and disgust pertaining to the "immature idiots who call themselves the students of the Academic Opportunity Program." After what seemed like an eternity, the halt of the elevator signaled its doors to open. As the two professors exited, the odor of their disgust changed to the stench of their laughter and mockery. I stayed in the elevator, feeling much

like the elevator operators of old – always along for the ride, but with no destination. The following day I began using the stairs; I had somewhere to go.

After twenty-three weeks, two days, fifty minutes, and thirty-eight seconds, I proudly exited the Academic Opportunity Program. It had indeed served its purpose. I was officially a "regular" college student and therefore quite anxious to reclaim my place on the elevator. As for the two professors, I remember eventually feeling sorry for them. It was obvious that they no longer shared in the excitement of their students' successes.

As my first year in college ended, I reflected on my experiences with a very positive feeling. I had several new friends: Twiddles, Ronald McBon, Larenzo, James, Doug, Becky, and Al. Their real names were Dan, Rick, Larry, Jaimie, Steve, Michelle and Alice. I always chose nicknames for my friends. It was my way of identifying them as people who were special to me.

By assuming the role of the "Artful Dodger," I usually managed to avoid courses reputed for their high level of difficulty. Some courses, however, were mandatory and inescapable. I kept a low profile in those courses to avoid the undesirable recurrence of my attempt at creativity in Mrs. Lark's class.

The time had come to detach myself from the parental shadow of dormitory life. Its lurking influence had given off-campus living an inviting appeal. I pictured myself in a home similar to the home I had shared with my parents, but the financial editor of "Life in the Real World" quickly deleted that page of my dream book.

Twiddles and I decided to share the upstairs portion of a house in the student ghetto. The two-story dilapidated home, otherwise known as 720 West Howard Street, was immediately christened, "The Roach Motel." The last segment of *Twilight Zone: The Movie* was mild compared to this infested nightmare; it reminded me of an insect version of Alfred Hitchcock's *The Birds*.

Hoping paint could mask deterioration, we quickly struggled to create a compromise between my parents' home and a dump. Success is in the eye of the beholder, but we eventually became quite comfortable with our new abode. I suppose our enthusiasm married our independence and provided a dazzling slipcover of optimism to our decision to move off-campus. Snow snuck into our bedroom; newspaper comics wallpapered our bathroom; loud music heated our living room, and dirty dishes decorated our kitchen, but we loved our place and probably would not have traded it for the most glamorous dormitory or fraternity house on the entire Ball State campus.

In the first four weeks of my second year, I went through three different majors. Initially I chose radio and television, which led me to journalism. My third and final choice was music. I guess I enjoyed the power of being in control of my future and therefore seized the moment by using my options as a new-found play toy. Being a music major was important: I had a briefcase for my music. Being a music major was demanding: I could not practice the piano in one of the many aisles of the student bookstore.

Halfway through the following school year, I realized what I loved most about music: its passion, clarity, and individuality. The most rewarding aspect of music was that the performer controlled its quality, be it good or bad. It was for that reason I felt I must drop music as a major and begin to experience my love for it once again. It was an extremely difficult decision. I even switched my instrumental focus to guitar in hopes of giving myself a fresh outlook, but the underlying feeling hauntingly remained. I was now confronted with a new nightmare. I was approximately one year away from a college degree, yet I had no goals, only obstacles. I had taken some courses in music therapy and done quite well, but I could not help but feel that for me to become a music therapist would be similar to a gourmet chef working in a cafeteria. It was at this point in my college career I realized that although my courses in the Department of Education were few, they were fun. I declared a major in education with absolutely no intention of ever becoming a teacher. I thought I knew what a teacher is, and is not. I realized I had a passion for education and also a fear of becoming what a teacher is not. I had to face the facts; I was destined to become a "professional college student." I even began to be very good at it. After all, I had counselors in five different departments of study.

Once I decided on a definite academic path, my confidence escalated, and, with the careful guidance of a few gifted professors, my writing skills improved; I started to actually enjoy writing papers and essays. Finally, I had overcome the horror of Mrs. Lark's stern dissertation on "the use of big words that you really don't know the meaning of." The days of the Academic Opportunity Program became increasingly insignificant, and I realized that my academic performance in the past was limited only by my own inhibitions. My papers became more and more cohesive, and their comments from my professors became more and more encouraging. I realized then the importance of encouragement: a poor student could very well be a brilliant individual who has never received a word of praise from his or her parents and teachers. This was a concept that I vowed to preserve if I was to become a teacher.

College

Things were a little better than perfect. I was absorbing an incredible amount of information and taking it very seriously. I was even persuaded by the propaganda of the moment. The educational system needed me. I did not know how, why, where, or when until I was instructed to spend the remaining twelve weeks of my final year in college as a student teacher in a middle school's resource room, working with students with learning disabilities. My supervising teacher was to be Mrs. Campbell.

STUDENT TEACHING 1981

Ronald Reagan wins presidential election
Assassination of Anwar Sadat
MTV debuts
Acquired Immune Deficiency Syndrome

When I first arrived in Mrs. Campbell's classroom, it was both quiet and dark. The lights were off, and the room was empty. I observed the classroom to be just as dark even after I turned the lights on. There were three items on Mrs. Campbell's desk: a large stack of ditto masters, a rubber glove tarnished with ditto fluid, and a Bible. The cover of the Bible was scarred with use, but there were peculiar signs of newness in the remainder of the Book. With the exception of the cover, the Bible seemed untouched, yet the ditto masters were used to the point of ineffectiveness — possibly in the literal sense. During this initial three minute introductory period, my wandering eyes were suddenly interrupted by a sound I had not heard since eighth grade English class. It was the sound of material rubbing together. Somehow I knew it was Mrs.

Campbell coming down the hallway.

The uncomfortable grimace she displayed was necessitated by her tightly coiffed bun. Within the first few exchanges of congenialities, however, I felt it was necessary to reassess my observations. The beaded sweat of her forehead, coupled with her lack of breath, shifted my attention to her size and heel height. As she grooved a direct path to her desk, she asked me about myself, only to interrupt my reply with what proved to be the missing link to her mysterious desktop. She used the Bible as a stability guide to her seat and as an aid to her teaching strategies. As her posterior found the desk chair, she stated, ". . . And Tim, while I'm thinking about it, could you please get one of the secretaries in the office to show you how to use the ditto machine? I'm going to need twenty-eight copies of each of these before the students arrive tomorrow morning. You may want to have them issue you your own glove."

If Mrs. Campbell was indeed one of the dreaded "Ditto Queens," then I was about to become the "Ditto King." I prepared huge folders for each student consisting of a week's worth of ditto sheets for each subject. My role was to make sure the students completed each of them without talking and to be sure they made all of the corrections after I had checked them. Her role was to abruptly slam her hand down on the Bible as a startling attention getter and reprimand the talker while firmly holding the hand of God. At the conclusion of the twelve weeks, my final grade was to be 70% from Mrs. Campbell and 30% from my college supervisor. My grade from Mrs. Campbell depended on my hair length, religious beliefs, and whether or not I would brush my teeth daily. I received extra credit when I would dash for donuts before school began each morning. On the other hand, the grade from my college

supervisor depended on my observational reports, creating and implementing an entire instructional unit, interaction with the students, teaching skills, attendance, and my overall attitude toward my role. Every time Mrs. Campbell began to drown me, my college supervisor was there to toss me a life preserver. In fact, it was his comment that kept me afloat, "You know Tim, sometimes you can learn just as much from a bad teacher as you can from a good one. As with your entire teaching career, your student teaching experience will become what you make it."

I learned many things from Mrs. Campbell, none of which I really cared for. She represented what a teacher is not. The most valuable lesson I learned from Mrs. Campbell was to avoid all the things she did as a teacher. I realized I had to be a teacher to do this. If for no other reason, I had to be a teacher to make sure there was a choice for students and their parents — a choice between what a teacher is and is not. I suppose my college supervisor was right. I received an "A" in student teaching and a brand new Bible. Then I let my hair grow.

It was graduation day at Ball State University. My formal educational career was over. The innocence of Jefferson Elementary School, the fears of Joy Elementary School, the traumas of Elston Junior High, the avoidance of Rogers Senior High, and the rewards of college had all become the past. It was this influential past that would now be credited to the future. My college degree meant a lot to me, and yet I did not have the overwhelming feeling of pride I felt I should have. My parents did, and so did my loving wife, Mary Beth. I, however, did not. I was not ready to teach. Maybe I felt inadequate, perhaps unprepared. Maybe I was not ready to grow up and become a professional or "model" citizen. Maybe my later educational experiences were not fulfilling enough and I felt the desire to recapture what was rightfully mine. It may have been for all of these reasons – it may have been for none, but I chose to pursue a master's degree in, of course, education.

I would like to think it was my scholastic aptitude that landed my graduate assistantship, but an overall 2.6 GPA from my undergraduate studies terminated that idea. Out of many applicants, only four received assistantships to the Department of Special Education. Maybe I had the proper mixture of luck and ambition for the award. Ironically, the professor I was to assist was Dr. Meyers, who was also my student teaching supervisor. I wanted to believe he recognized my potential and educational hunger and felt this would be a way to feed it.

When I was not checking materials in and out of the Student Resources Center, I was busy doing research on whether or not family members of Down's syndrome children had webbed toes. This research topic proved to me one of two things: either Dr. Meyers stood in some bad wind and allowed his pilot light to go out, or he had absolutely nothing else for me to do. As I grew to know him better, I kind of felt he was simply not dealt a full deck, which, in essence, brought me back to the dilemma of what a teacher is and is not.

Within twelve months I had a master's degree and was extremely proud. I remember being in a grocery store and wondering why all of the people were not as elated as I was. I had not experienced those feelings since the birth of my first son. I even went through the commencement exercises this time, complete with robe and hood. I learned more in one year of post-graduate work than in four years of undergraduate studies. I had fabulous professors, and I admired their preparatory skills. Dr. Clark taught the course, Learning

Disabilities: Theory and Practice. The first day of class he handed all of his students the final exam. He exclaimed, "As lengthy as this exam may seem, this is your course final exam. Anything and everything I want you to learn in this class will be assessed on this final exam. You will be responsible to return this to me on the last day of class, at which time I will immediately hand it back to you as your final exam. I am not hung up on motivation, exams, statistics, curves, and course grades, but I am hung up on knowledge and learning. You will learn everything in this course. You will learn everything worthy of my teaching." I guess he reminded me of Mr. Williams from my high school days.

I borrowed Dr. Clark's philosophy of learning and never bothered to return it. The thrill of achievement and being reminded once again of what a teacher is, pushed many past negative educational experiences to one side and eventually under me. Therefore, the stage was set for me to become a teacher, so that I might trample and grind those experiences under my new found outlook. The children had obviously been ready for quite some time. Now, I was ready also. A few days prior to graduation, I accepted a teaching position with a large school district in Houston, Texas, working with elementary children with learning disabilities. Driving the twenty-four foot moving truck off the university campus with my three month old son strapped in tight, I looked in the side mirror of my imagination and saw Mrs. Towers. She was much older, and she was smiling. As I slowed the truck to thank her, her image faded . . . and she was gone. I knew that in 1963, when she first put a welcome grasp on my hand, she had never let it go. At times her grip loosened, but she never let it go. My tension eased as I realized that she was going with me to Houston and would always stand before the children next to me. I understood what Robert Fulghum meant when he said, "All I ever really needed to know I learned in kindergarten." And so, as some things end, others begin.

THE EDUCATIONAL POST

Daily, weekly, and for the rest of your life - with summers off

Price: ~$50,000 (total tuition)   August 12, 1982

DEATHS

Mark Lee Walding, departed the teaching world on August 12, 1982. A native educator, Mr. Walding was a graduate of the Model All-American High School and received his B.S. in math and science at the United States Teacher's College. After a brief illness which resulted in a craving for the corporate world, Mr. Walding's desire to teach expired. He is survived by his colleagues, the P.T.A., his students, and their children. In lieu of the usual remembrances the family requests donations to the "National Society for the Preservation of Teachers" (NSPT). At Mr. Walding's final request, there will be no services. May he invest in peace.

BIRTHS

Mr. and Mrs. David F. Gangwer are pleased to announce the birth of their teacher, Timothy P. Gangwer, born at 5:36 p.m. on August 12, 1982, at Ball State University in Muncie, Indiana. Timothy had the weight, height, and I.Q. equivalent to a B.S. degree and an M.A. in Education. He has understanding eyes and an indistractible presence. Students, parents, friends, and relatives are invited to visit academe's bundle of joy.

FIRST
TEACHING
ASSIGNMENT
1982

Vietnam Veteran's Memorial Wall
E.T.
Michael Jackson's *Thriller*
Princess Grace of Monaco dies
American Marines in Beirut
Manuel Noriega
Lee Iacocca
America's Cup

As the constant hum of the truck's tires mingled with the coo and occasional cry of my infant son, I began to manifest some occupational anxieties. Where will I teach? Will I be what a teacher is? Will the students like me? The intimidating threat of change continually chased my thoughts only to catch them, press them, and turn them loose to resume wandering and wondering with my emotions. It was already a long drive, but for each mile traveled there became an additional half-mile of anxieties.

My teaching assignment lay quietly in a patient envelope at our new apartment. I opened it even before opening the back of the moving truck. I was given the assignment of a resource room special education teacher in an elementary school. It was an inner-city school, complete with tall chain-link fences topped with barbed-wire. It was located in the city's Fifth Ward – an area known for its high level of poverty and corresponding high crime rate. The ethnic breakdown of the five-hundred-twenty-student population consisted of somewhere around 85% black, 10% Hispanic, and the remaining 5% were simply listed as "other."

I chose to give myself a tour of the neighborhood and school grounds prior to my first day at the school. There was an overwhelming air of poverty and one-room "shotgun" houses, strategically unbalanced on cinderblocks. Homes that had burned lay in a crumpled pile of charred memories scenting the neighborhood. Empty lots harboring rodents and sidewalks consumed with weeds speckled every block. In spite of my intimidation and distress, I noticed the children. Most were barefoot and many appeared dirty and unkempt, but happy. They romped and played with the universal innocence that all children share. This observation served as a temporary diversion and added a thought provoking balance to everything else I had seen.

The school was sandwiched between the remains of a city park and the Coke Street Apartments, where many of the schoolchildren lived. I remember wondering if that were a drug-related nickname for the dwelling, or if it was actually located on a street named "Coke." The park had several children utilizing the area, which had once been the home of brightly colored playground equipment. It was littered with several people protectively nursing a concealed beverage in a plain brown wrapper. As a future teacher, I could not help but dwell on the unfortunate role-modeling habits of these people. Although children appear to be quite busy with play, they remain very perceptive. The eyes and ears of a child often become the victim of an adult's ignorance.

The school was in slight disrepair. The parking lot was mainly gravel with the exception of a small, paved strip highlighted with a bold fluorescent paint proclaiming "PRINCIPAL." Truthfully, I was glad to be one of the "gravel people." As I drove around to the rear of the building, I saw what had the appearance of another residential house on cinderblocks, but this particular structure was connected to the rear door of the school building by what was once a concrete sidewalk. There were large boarded squares where air-conditioners once functioned. The windows were covered by a thick wire mesh. Under the shack was a dark and damp crawlspace with an inviting, yet dangerous lure to the children. I remember relying on my humor to control the moment by thinking, "Well Tim, looks like you found your first classroom. How do you like it?"

As I headed out of the neighborhood, I began to feel sorry for myself. I had a master's degree in education, motivation, and a new teacher ambition; yet I was going to have to teach in a school notorious for two things: The district paid any teacher who dared to assume an assignment at this particular school a stipend of $2,000, and the teachers were given instructions not to be in the neighborhood after sundown. Reflecting on my thoughts at that particular moment, I can assess them as being very self-centered. I assumed that I had earned my way into what one might consider the model, all-American school – a selfish, yet understandable attitude for a college

graduate. This attitude even began to shadow the anxieties I had been experiencing as a first-year teacher. Regardless of what I felt I had earned, I was to report to the school by 8:00 a.m. on the following day.

TEACHING

Finally, the big day had come. I will never forget hopping out of bed early to take my morning shower. Everything that day seemed new and unique. I tried to scrub away those feelings of worry and disappointment. I cannot remember what I ate for breakfast; I guess maybe my anticipation interrupted my hunger. My clothes were new and stiff, and they made noise when I walked. They smelled just like the store I bought them from, and I checked my shirt for stray pins. My shoes were so shiny that I could see the clouds in the tops of them. The minutes seemed like seconds as I drove to school.

When I arrived, the building had changed drastically overnight. It had grown to three times its normal size. It was breathing in and out. Children were gripping the fence while peering at me with questioning eyes. I answered their eyes with a smile. As I turned the car off, I felt somewhat confused. I had the horrifying feeling that I was the sacrificial lamb. I clung tightly to a spiral notebook, a pencil, and my car keys as I approached the building.

Then it happened. As I walked closer to the door, which was eight stories tall, the building took a ghastly surge of breath and sucked me in. It was very powerful. The building was hungry that day. There were other helpless teachers desperately clinging to their notebooks. I joined them in hiding my fears behind an artificial smile.

That is when I saw her for the first time. She did not really look much like somebody's mom. She had a deceptively sweet voice with a matching smile, and she was very congenial. As her eyebrows danced with the inflection of her voice, she helped to sprinkle a touch of self-confidence on my anxieties and fears. While I anxiously awaited my first tour of the building and the introduction to my first career classroom, I was issued my teaching supplies.

This was to be the year of the canvas supply bag. It was bright white with a bold red apple silkscreened on one side. The apple was as red as a polished fire engine. Although it was exactly the same as the other teachers' bags, it was much different — it was mine. It belonged to me, the new teacher on the block. The contents were priceless: a heavy metallic stapler that gleamed in the light from the windows, two fine-point pens that had the rare quality of having their caps intact, and a box of untouched, ghost-white chalk, eagerly waiting to be converted into educational dust.

As Mrs. Ross, the principal, emerged from her mysterious office door (teachers were not allowed behind the front office counter), my excitement began to build because I knew I was moments away from viewing my first classroom — Mr. Gangwer's classroom, to be exact. As we began our journey down the hall, she commented on how glossy the halls were and how the custodial staff was committed to a clean building. I had a different perspective. I noticed how the fluorescent lights reflected on the freshly waxed hallway floors, giving the appearance of a sparkling bracelet. Also, I wondered if I would have been able to see the lights reflected in the tops of my shoes had they not been scuffed from the gravel parking lot. We had reached the farthest point of the building and still had not diverted to a vacant room. As the rear door swung

First Teaching Assignment

open, I saw what was once a concrete sidewalk. We headed in the direction of the Coke Street Apartments and stopped at what was now described to me as not only the "T-Shack" or Temporary Building, but also . . . my first classroom. I was handed a key to a door that would not lock and told that I could have anything I needed. My foreshadowing derision of the dilapidated shed the day before suddenly lost its humor. I stood in the doorway holding my canvas supply bag, which had grayed in color and grown quite heavy. The building was dark, dirty, and full of unwanted discards, which the school refused to officially throw away. About the only real signs of life were the cockroaches and the burnt matches that lay in the aftermath of a child's curiosity with fire. It was the pile of matches that sparked my optimism. It made me review the value of a childhood fort. Children had reserved this small building as their secret hideaway, and it was my job to dress it up and turn it into a learning environment while maintaining its allure as a fort. I welcomed the challenge and privately thanked the young trespassers. I decided that since it was a different building, it should therefore have a separate name. It was, after all, mine. I began to grow proud of "Gangwer Elementary School."

As time passed, I really enjoyed the children. They had a defined appreciation for the small things. What was a new bicycle for some was a new pencil for others. I enjoyed distributing pencils for that very reason. One night, all of my teaching materials were stolen. The school district's security grilled the students to no avail. Class continued as usual at Gangwer Elementary for two days, and I never mentioned the theft to my students. I continued the instruction with my new make-shift materials. On the third day, all of the stolen materials mysteriously reappeared at my doorway. The students asked if they could take my new make-shift materials home since I would no longer be needing them. How could I resist.

During an academically oriented card game, the students and I were caught up in some rhyming patterns. For example: "blue, blue, pass to you; yellow, yellow, feelin' mellow; red, red, you heard what I said." My surprise came with the straight-faced contribution of Derrick, "Green, green, yo' bootie ain't clean." I was caught off guard to the point of literally falling off the chair and onto the floor with laughter. The best part was the other students looked at me as if I were insane and simply could not understand where I had found the humor. I learned to moonwalk like Michael Jackson and heard the stories of gunshots lulling the children to sleep each night. I learned to "rap," and I saw the children who wore the same clothes each day, minus the traditional zippers and buttons. I learned the official rules of trash can basketball and heard he rumbling sounds of small stomachs. I even began to feel guilty about going home to an air-conditioned apartment and the securing caress of my family.

At the close of my first teaching year, I approached two students who were engaged in a racial dispute. One student was black and the other white. It was spring. I saw clenched fists and angry faces. I was quick to put my past experiences between them. As I began to slowly let the air out of their ballooning tension, the black student revealed, "This honkey shoved me for no reason!" My first inquiry was in reference to what a "honkey" was. He replied, "You know, a white dude." I then asked him if, since I was white, did that make me a "honkey" also. His smile highlighted his response, "Aw Mr. Gangwer, you're not white . . . you're a teacher!" I was fascinated by his image of a teacher. As for the minor racial confrontation, the two students unclenched their fists and released their anger. It was obvious that the two students recognized ethnic differences between themselves, but I wondered at what age they would begin to recognize the ethnic differences in their teachers. Regardless of my thoughts at the time, I guess I really appreciated not belonging to any ethnic group during those impressionably brief moments. I was placed in a group unique only to the perceptions of a child: the teaching race.

During the course of the following school year, my attention was stolen from the children as I was force-fed the startling habits of the school administration. They abused important priorities and displayed blatant favoritism. I was one of the favored teachers and still felt the unmistakable tremor of the faculty's negative vibrations. The most critical element of the administration, which eventually influenced my transfer to a new school, was the excessive and inappropriate (ab)use of corporal punishment. I saw teachers who carried steel-edge rulers, frequently used to slap the bare calf of a child for talking in the hallway while awaiting a turn at the drinking fountain. As the victim would slowly lift up a pant leg while rolling down a sock in anticipation of the stinging crack of the ruler, I would hear the teacher say, "I'm sorry about this darlin'. You know I love you and want you to be right." Other teachers did not feel a paddling was effective unless they could see the lifting soles of the children's shoes from the force of the blows. The principal did not necessarily approve of such disciplinary measures, but she was definitely aware of them. A young third grade teacher asked me to witness a paddling, which was to be administered in accordance with the district's policy. When I entered her room, I observed seven pitiful children, glassy-eyed with fear. After removing

First Teaching Assignment

the lump in my throat, I asked the teacher what the students had done. She replied, "Well Mr. Gangwer, as a matter of fact, it is what they have not done. It seems they decided to forget to bring their homework today!" After refusing to witness the atrocity, I confronted the teacher with the challenge of adopting an incentive program, as opposed to the habitual rut of corporal punishment. "These kids are used to extension cords! A couple of whacks on the bottom won't kill 'em. Besides, this is the only form of discipline they know," she quickly protested. That incident gave me seven sound reasons to transfer. At the close of the school year, our principal was feted as the district's "Principal of the Year." It was then I realized the deception of her smile. As the sounds of applause filled her ears, my ears were hauntingly filled with the sound of wood against small pockets. While I packed my belongings, I felt sorry for the principal and promptly placed her in the elevator with the two professors from the Academic Opportunity Program. Naturally, the elevator was going down. I often think about the children gripping the fence while peering at me with questioning eyes. I feel sorry that I am no longer there to answer them with my smile. I gave them my smile on the very first day of my teaching career. I hope they kept it.

Although it was a sigh of relief, I could not help but feel that I had abandoned the students who needed me most. Adults often tend to favor the cute child – what one might describe as "clean-cut" and "from a nice family." Unfortunately, those children may not be the ones who need the favoring. The child with an unkempt appearance, or an unhealthy look, or a constant runny nose is the child least likely to be favored, and yet perhaps the most needy. I like to think that I favored several needy children my first two years of teaching.

GANGWER ELEMENTARY: NEWLY RELOCATED 1984

Los Angeles Olympics
Bishop Desmond Tutu
Live Aid
Mikhail Gorbachev
Chicago Bears
Titanic is found
Challenger disaster
Muammar Qaddafi
Oliver North and the Iran-contra trials
Chernolbyl Meltdown
Black Monday
Baby Jessica
The fall of Jim and Tammy Bakker
George Bush wins presidential election
***From Both Sides of the Desk* is published**

Gangwer Elementary

If the model all-American school did actually exist, then I had found it. Located in the heart of a neighborhood where doctors and lawyers mingled their salaries with the school's materials budget, the organization of the Kolter Elementary School administration represented many of the teaching and behavioral philosophies I had looked for in my first assignment. It was not the community, its economy, or the location of the school that impressed me, it was the overall effect these variables had on the genuine quality of the school. There was, of course, a certain degree of culture shock, but I had acquired a gift from my previous students; by not associating students with any particular race, I could place them in a group unique only to the perception of a teacher: the student race.

I had a wonderful, brightly lit classroom that had a scenic view of the frolicking antics of the playground people, as opposed to the ornate chain-link/barbed-wire combination. Kolter Elementary was a school within a school within a school. It contained the School of International Culture and, of course, Gangwer Elementary — newly relocated. Reminiscent of my college friends, I issued each one of my new students a nickname, which they joyfully acknowledged as a humorous honor. Corey became *Alphonzo;* Juan became *"J.J.";* Todd became *Eddie Haskell;* Jennifer became *Wanita;* Larry Cheeseton became *Cheddar;* Terry Cheeseton became *Mozzarella;* Michael became *The Moses Man;* Benjamin became *Pancake;* Stephanie became *Spatula;* Francine became *Franyard;* and Daniel became *The Big "D."* I quickly found the students really depended on established routines, but routines can become very mundane. Therefore, I chose to toss a little spice on a rather bland, but important part of our daily menu. The nicknames sparked an ongoing fun way to take attendance each day or introduce class members to classroom visitors.

Lining up for lunch is exciting in a delicious sort of way, but this too can grow old. Thus, it became necessary to write our own song to sing as we lined up: "Oh ... we ... will (clap) strap on the grazing bags (clap), strap on the grazing bags (clap), strap on the grazing bags, and we will (clap) strap on the grazing bags when we go to lunch, (hip thrust) UH!" I must confess, it was rare when we actually got all the way through it without having to peel our laughter-limp bodies off the floor.

Listening to a teacher during the day can get a bit tedious at times — that is, unless the teacher has a built-in word the students recognize as a signal for a predetermined, choral response. Therefore, anytime the students would hear me say the word "if" followed by a brief pause, they would immediately respond with a choral, "you know what I'm saying." It was rare when all of my students with so-called, auditory perception problems would miss an "if" (pause), "you know what I'm saying."

Once again, I was teaching a special education class, but this particular class was self-contained. It was known in the district as a "generic classroom." The term "generic" refers to the fact that the class consisted of a melting pot of disabled students. They were either learning disabled, mentally handicapped, emotionally handicapped, orthopedically handicapped, and/or speech handicapped. All of the students shared the commonality of functioning at least one year behind their expected level. I suppose someone deemed it practical to call it a generic classroom. Personally, I think of the phrase, "Label soup cans, not children," and I am therefore reminded that there are generic soup brands. I have often toyed with the idea of asking my students to dress all in white and list their bodily ingredients on the back of their shirts. Regardless of its title, the generic classroom presented what I felt to be the ultimate teaching challenge. Here were ten students from different cultural backgrounds, with individual learning deficits and styles, and with varying functional levels. It sounds overwhelming, but it was actually intriguing. I had the invigorating task of first finding out what was causing this large gap between what they were learning and what they should have been learning, and then locating a prescriptive strategy to arm their strengths by attacking their weaknesses. As the weaknesses fell at the mighty hand of success, the strengths would begin to clutter the narrowing gap, which originally defined the learning deficit. At that point, I would begin to mainstream the students by including them, one subject at a time, in regular education classes. The ultimate goal was to eventually mainstream them on a full-time basis. This, of course, was the success story. Mrs. Towers and I are proud to say that out of ten original students, only three remained in my class by the end of the year. I am told that many self-contained education classes do not exercise the goal of mainstreaming. I feel this is a mistake. As I tell my students, a learning difficulty simply means that a person does not learn in the same fashion as many other students. If two students walk around the block side by side, but one student constantly zips in and out of bushes, around houses, up and down trees, and over fences, one thing remains the same: both students will eventually end up in the same place. The shortest route between two points is always a straight line, but not necessarily the only route. As the learning disabled student is busy zipping in and out of bushes, around houses, up and down trees, and over fences, one can imagine what the average student is missing by staying on the sidewalk. I give my students a lot of credit, but I also maintain high expectations.

By the time I had settled in at Kolter, I began taking notice of some of the teaching issues that had not been as prevalent before. I realized that the single most important aspect of preparing for daily lessons was never to be prepared. Spontaneity became the unique element of my teaching style, which allowed me the opportunity to sponge every drop of creativity out of the students. Planning became nothing more than a vehicle to ensure the presentation of all subjects throughout the day. I tried to adhere to the district policies of preparing and planning, but found myself constantly preparing to plan and planning to prepare a plan worthy of preparatory planning. Eventually, I found the best plan was to prepare to be myself, be what a teacher is, and try to do that perfectly. After all, it would be hypocritical for me to set such high expectations for my students and not for myself.

Mr. Williams, my high school government teacher with the bushy-eyebrowed assertiveness, taught me the formula for what a teacher is (one part Horace Mann and one part Johnny Carson). Today, I completely understand the validity of his formula, particularly since teachers are constantly competing with the magical world of video games and the adventurous world of skateboarding. I have begun to realize that if I entertain students while utilizing educational elements as my stand-up material, they will not only learn, but also have fun while doing so. A good teacher is mostly an entertainer in one way or another — an entertainer who channels the attention of his students by transposing subject matter into daily fun. A little teaching mingled with a lot of entertainment provides an exciting learning environment. In contrast, a lot of teaching with little or no entertainment value fosters a sterile classroom full of apathetic minds. There are a variety of fabulous ways to approach any task; one of them is to select strategies that play to personal strengths and individual interests. For example: instead of, "Johnny had five apples. Kimberly ate two of Johnny's apples. How many apples did Johnny have left?" how about, "As the five brave Ninjas began their quest, they were suddenly ambushed by the feared Skunk People. Although they fought bravely, three Ninjas were taken hostage. Your adventure begins by planning their escape, but you must first determine how many of the original five warriors you have left to take with you. Good Luck!" As you might suspect, Ninjas and Skunk People have many more attractive qualities than Johnny and Kimberly's apples. Apples rot; adventure ripens. Instead of wading through a story problem, the students are challenged to go on a mathematical quest through the mystical world of subtraction.

If the students ever grow tired of me, I leave the classroom and bring someone else back to do the teaching, such as Michael Jackson. I simply step out of the room, pull a few strands of hair over my forehead, don a single white glove, and moonwalk right back into the room. After the laughter subsides, their attention is mine. They do not dare risk missing something worthy of their entertainment.

Perceptions

THE CHILD'S EYE

I remember living in a relatively large house as a child. My family would journey to the country for what seemed to take hours. We would purchase a bushel of freshly picked apples from the orchard. I loved the overwhelming aroma of our car as we headed home. The apples were always fresh and crisp, and the bite of a fresh apple had a unique sound. The sounds and smells of the apples would be present for many days as a reminder of the journey and our orchard adventure.

Today as I drive past my childhood home, I smile at the small, quaint house which once seemed relatively large. I suppose the house grew smaller as I grew larger. I have learned that what may be a cloudy day to an adult, could very well be a severe thunderstorm to a child. What may be an annoying weed to an adult, may be a towering tree to a child. What may be sloppy, careless work to a teacher, may be a magnificent effort to a student. I make it a point to analyze my childhood perceptions to accommodate the perceptions of my students. Every day, I smell the wonderful aroma and hear the crisp bite of a fresh apple in my classroom.

I make it a point to let my students know a teacher does not know everything. I am not infallible. Students tend to create a major league image of teachers who are really in the minor league. It is beneficial for students to enjoy and respect their teachers; they should realize, however, that they do not always have all the answers. I have devised a list of questions designed to stimulate the humorous wheels of a student's mind. They will accentuate my point in a fun fashion:

Why does your mom say, "If I told you once, I told you a thousand times. . ." when she really only told your twice.

Why would your dad say, "You're walking on thin ice, Pal!" and it's the middle of July?

If your dad says, "People just aren't what they used to be," does that mean he has met everyone?

What do you do at dinner when your dad tells you, "Just close your mouth and eat"?

Is a math drill a power tool?

Does paying attention drain your savings account?

How do you join hands in a circle if you are square dancing?

After reading a story, how can you be expected to draw conclusions if you are not artistic?

How can you get straight "A's" if your teacher grades on a curve?

Is special ed. related to Mr. Ed?

If someone has a "private eye," does that mean no one is allowed to look at it?

If all seven castaways landed at the same time, why was it called "Gilligan's Island"?

Perceptions

How is a nutcracker sweet, and who tasted it?

Why is it dangerous to let a friend ride on the handlebars of your unicycle?

How do you really know if a bottomless pit is actually bottomless?

If you tear a bookworm, can you mend it with a tapeworm?

Do you have to clean your shoes after a cake walk?

Does earwax melt?

Should you ever lie quietly in bed if you've been told to always tell the truth?

Why don't cold-hearted people just put on a sweater?

Can you "get a kick" out of something without getting a bruise?

If "one good turn deserves another," does it ever stop?

Can a bottle-nose dolphin ever get kicked in the can?

Is there a separate section of heaven for bedwetters?

Do you "get the blues" from a combination of getting the greens and yellows?

Children enjoy fun and laughter, but they do not always enjoy thinking. This list tends to stimulate all three. The human senses become dull when they are not adequately exercised on a daily basis. Exercising can be tiresome, yet one never tires of exercising one of the most important senses of all: the sense of humor.

Being both a parent and a teacher has been very beneficial. It has allowed me to assess the arena of a child's emotional and social traits from a ringside seat. Children display certain personality traits in the comfort of their home environment that they would never dream of revealing at school. Therefore, there may be many sides of a child that the teacher simply does not have an opportunity to observe. I suppose this is true of adults as well. I am convinced there are several adult personality traits which do not surface at the office, but are frequently seen by family members at home.

As the school year progresses, children begin feeling some of the comforts of the home environment while at school. I cannot begin to count the many times students have mistakenly called me "mom" or "dad." I usually reward their feelings of comfort by responding, regardless of their error.

When my own children discuss their school experiences over dinner, I frequently make mental notes. As a teacher, I use my notes to achieve a better understanding of my students' perceptions of their daily school experiences.

Establishing parent/teacher partnerships is actually a pleasure, as opposed to an intimidating chore. During parent conferences it is difficult to avoid comments like, "I know exactly what you mean," or "That happens at my house all the time." I feel parents appreciate my dual role and coinciding perceptions. In fact, they are often prompted to express their sympathy. I explain to each parent that teaching and parenting are similar in some ways, but much different in other ways. For example, just about the time parents figure out the behavioral characteristics of their eight year old, the child has a birthday and the behavioral quest of the parent begins all over again. Whereas, a teacher generally deals with one age group and one grade level. I try to convey some of these observations to parents when conducting yearly conferences. I also keep a record of the humorous antics and outstanding achievements of each student throughout the year. My documentation creates an opportunity for me to steal a smile from each parent when they're not looking. Also, to ensure the parents leave their tension and anxiety outside the classroom door, I ask each of my students to bring a complete set of their own clothing to school one day prior to parent conference day. The students stuff their clothing with newspaper and paint a self-portrait on a stuffed paper bag to place on the shoulders of their scarecrows. The parents truly enjoy seeing a classroom full of imitation students seated in the desks. I fondly refer to them as "my academically inclined dummies."

THE TWENTY-FOUR HOUR, NEGATIVE TO POSITIVE CONVERSION CHART FOR PARENTS AND TEACHERS

The following conversion chart is designed to instill peace of mind into parents of schoolchildren everywhere. The correct use of the chart consists of twisting a child's words to make them more pleasing to the parental ear. The child's statement is listed first, followed by the suggested parent response. The goal of the conversion chart is to promote and maintain a varying degree of sanity. Teachers are encouraged to utilize the chart between the hours of 8:00 a.m. and 3:00 p.m.

TIME	OFFSPRING
6:45 a.m.	I'm not gonna go to school today . . . I'm sick.
6:46	I feel better.
7:00	You didn't get milk on all the pieces of cereal.
7:15	You didn't pick out my clothes.
7:30	Do I gotta make my bed?
7:45	Is there a surprise in my lunch?

	STUDENT
8:00	Why do we gotta say the Pledge?
8:05	When can I go to the bathroom?
8:06	Suzie looked at me!
8:15	Is it lunchtime yet?
9:30	Why do we gotta do reading stuff?

PARENT'S RESPONSE

It must be because your last vaccination didn't work. I had better call Dr. Bob to set another appointment.

You look much better.

After you finish eating, it will all be mixed very nicely in your stomach.

You have my permission to go to school naked.

No, the furniture company did that for you, but I would like you to tuck in your sheets and blankets.

Yes, there are no Twinkies.

TEACHER'S RESPONSE

Was there something else you wanted to say instead?

After you have given your bladder adequate time to fill.

I will call her parents tonight.

Yes, but we are running about two hours behind schedule today.

I want to make sure you are able to read the instructions to video games.

Perceptions

9:35	Cindy looked at me!
9:55	Why do we gotta learn this junk?
11:00	Why do we gotta always be washing our hands before lunch?
11:05	Why didn't mom put Twinkies in my lunch?
11:40	Recess is too short!
12:20 p.m.	When is it time to go home?
1:15	I need a drink.
1:50	Don't you ever go to the bathroom?
2:25	Could we dissect a worm in science today?
2:55	Why do we gotta do homework?

OFFSPRING

3:30	Can I have a Twinkie?
4:15	I hate homework! It stinks!
5:30	I hate smash potatoes!

I will see that she is expelled.

So you will be able to recognize junk when you see it.

You don't. You have to find a way to make sure they never get dirty.

Because she likes me.

You have already learned everything there is to know about recess.

Sometime between lunch and dinner.

So do I . . . so do I.

Yes, but I never have time to use it.

No, you already did that during recess.

So I can spend my evenings grading papers.

PARENT'S RESPONSE

No, but would you like a snack instead?

Don't smell it, just do it.

Just try to think of them as hot ice cream you eat with a fork.

7:00	I don't wanna take a bath!
8:00	Why do I gotta brush my teeth all the time?
8:30	But why did the Big Bad Wolf eat Little Red Riding Hood's grandma?
8:59	I think I'm comin' down with something again, mom.
9:00	"Zzzzzzzzzzzz ..."
10:00 - 6:45 a.m.	"Zzzzzzzzzzzz ..."

Fine. Take a shower.

You don't. By the way, did I mention the dentist has a brand new drill?

Because she was always sick, never took a bath or brushed her teeth, and she ate Twinkies all the time.

I'll get some cod liver oil to help settle your stomach.

Whew!

"Zzzzzzzzzzzz . . ."

WHAT
IS A TEACHER?

In the Prologue of this book, I mentioned that teaching is a chain of events in our lives. As infants, we begin our lives learning to live. As we grow older, we find ourselves living to learn. As a child, I experienced the luxuries of learning along with the accompanying hindrances, but the most important aspect of all of my lifelong learning is that it has affected my teaching. I may not have realized it at the time, but I am now aware that everything I learned in school as a child, teenager, and young adult has ultimately had an effect on all of the children I have taught in the past, as well as all of the children I will teach in the future. Allowing my students the opportunity to inherit the good elements while avoiding the bad ones has become one of my constant concerns. I try to look more like somebody's dad, instead of looking like a teacher. I crouch down low enough to look into the eyes of a child as they speak to me. I always have patience with the child who cries for his mom on the first day of school. I marvel in amazement when a child describes the contents of his cigar box. I understand why it takes a child so long to walk alone down a freshly waxed hallway. I do not criticize children who question my teaching. I accept the fact that I will someday have loose skin. I know the difference between shaking a child's hand and shaking a child's body. I freely admit that love is blind at any age. I am patient with children who misbehave their first few days after transferring from another school, and I encourage children to give themselves a valentine each year. I never belittle children, and I try to ignore their messes. I always make a special effort to pass the football to every child at least once during a game, and I even allow my shirt tail to hang out occasionally. I never

question the child who wears the same shirt more than once during the week. If our school had a fire slide, my students and I would be forced to have weekly drills in the absence of an emergency. I tell the small children, "You're not too small — everyone else is too big!" I stress the importance of good, clear vision: "There is nothing wrong with your eyes, until you begin to notice a difference in skin color. Once this happens, even prescriptive glasses won't help. You will eventually grow blind with prejudice. Those are the only eyes you have. Protect them!" I explain to my students that self-esteem is not something someone gives you. Self-esteem is something you are born with, and you must learn to recognize and use it as an asset to your personality. I encourage children to welcome change into their lives. I do not talk *at* my students, I talk *with* them. I do not say things I think they want to hear, I say things I want to say. I am primarily concerned *that* they learn, and then *what* they learn. Recognizing and complimenting a child's success is like fueling the flame of a hot air balloon. The hotter the air, the higher the balloon will continue to rise. It is very rewarding for a teacher to stand and look up at the sky of success as it becomes cluttered with thousands of tiny colorful dots — too high to even recognize as hot air balloons. Finally, I encourage them to continue their ongoing search as to what a teacher is and is not, and to continue their search long after they think they have found that ideal.

Although the search is endless, I have established what I feel a teacher is, based on my own experiences and perceptions:

A TEACHER IS . . .

Someone who has the ability to control both their anger and their bladder, since there seems to be little time in the day for either.

Someone who is "real" and looks a lot like somebody's mom or dad.

Someone who has an open door policy, but usually keeps it shut to avoid disrupting other classes.

Someone who puts a light touch on heavy subjects.

Someone who understands why children cannot memorize multiplication tables, but have no difficulty memorizing the lyrics to Michael Jackson songs.

Someone who is always conscious of when the school day begins, but never conscious when it ends.

Someone who takes the failure of a child personally.

Someone who never tires of chasing a child's potential around a classroom.

Someone who can transform a worthless stick of limestone into a priceless wand of knowledge and refer to it as "chalk."

Someone who accepts everything based on its educational merit alone.

Perceptions

Someone who encourages children not to follow in his footsteps, but to make tracks of their own.

Someone who still enjoys the smell of a freshly printed worksheet, but no longer savors the taste of paste.

Someone who learns as much as he teaches.

Someone who never walks away from a garage sale empty-handed.

Someone who serves an equal helping of "praise pie" to all students and encourages them to come back for seconds.

Someone who awakes from a dead sleep in the middle of the night wondering if his students will score well on the test the following morning.

Someone who looks up words like "rhythm" and "license" in the dictionary when the students aren't looking.

Someone who hums the "Alphabet Song" on the way home from work.

Someone who has eyes in the back of his head and can see through walls.

Someone who will not allow children to "use the restroom," but will allow them to "visit the restroom."

Someone who invites an astronaut as a guest speaker for the class and introduces him as a former student.

Someone who knows when to paint the walls of self-esteem with reassuring strokes of confidence.

Someone who regards math, science, social studies, and language arts as nothing more than an excuse to have fun.

Someone who understands that children can see sound, touch the sky, taste air, smell fear, and hear colors.

Someone who polices the streets in the imaginary cities of a child's mind.

Someone who has more parents and children than any family in the world.

Someone whose refrigerator door remains a magnetized collage of student sentiment.

Someone who regards poor judgment as a signal for help.

Someone who realizes that although a skyscraper of confidence can be destroyed in a matter of seconds, it can take many years to rebuild.

Someone who has accumulated enough apples to alter the world's hunger problem.

Someone who recognizes the "student race" as one which ignores wealth, poverty, gender, and ethnicity.

Someone who proudly displays the daily chalk and ink stains of achievement on his clothing.

Someone who learns as much from the mistakes of others as he does from his own.

Someone who understands that the forest of learning has more than one path to follow.

Someone who exercises motivational skills by day and motivates exercising skills by night.

Someone who understands that a child who struggles may very well be an overachiever trapped in an underachiever's body.

Classroom management can be a horrific monster to some, while being a tame lamb to others. I believe in the old method of preventive maintenance. A little imaginative thought into the structure and organization of a classroom provides an atmosphere that discourages inappropriate behavior. If children are busy being challenged, it is unlikely they will find time to exhibit disruptive behavior. Granted, some children require more attention than others. Therefore, I use an additional strategy involving motivational incentive programs. Although many people have the preconceived notion that incentive programs are actually a form of bribery, I feel these programs are effective and necessary. According to a dictionary, "bribery" means to corrupt and influence by favors and is often associated with an unlawful act. Obviously, allowing a child to accumulate compliments and trade them in for Scratch-n-Sniff stickers bears no resemblance to bribery. Some children do not trust their own skills and find it difficult to find any gratification from their classroom achievements. These children begin to seek gratification in other areas, such as peer attention and approval. They feel that if their classmates laugh at them, they are accepted as one of the more popular students in the class. My alternative to bribery allows the students the opportunity to keep track of my compliments, which emphasizes something more positive. These compliments stimulate the learner to chart his points, which provides the incentive. He knows he will receive the sticker after he acquires the predetermined amount of points. This individualized system becomes much more gratifying than the occasional giggle of a classmate. In fact, given the opportunity to step back and look in yesterday's mirror, the child is often embarrassed by the laughter that was once the pleasing sound of acceptance.

One of my favorite classroom management techniques is to abruptly announce, "Okay buddy, you're done! I caught you this time and you're not going to wiggle out of it! Don't try to deny it either young man. I caught you being good and I advise you to march right up to my desk for a bonus sticker, right now! Do you understand me!?" Children love to get caught being good. I find when a child gets caught, other children begin to display the same behavior in hopes of being the next victim. On a group level, it never hurts to occasionally stop in the middle of a lesson with a startling, "Uh class, just what do you think you're doing? If you think for one minute that I would even consider standing up here while all of you are being good just any ol' time you please, then you have another think coming! Now I want every one of you to line up at that door for a little free play outdoors. Maybe next time you'll think twice before being good in this classroom!"

It would be unfair of me to avoid sharing what happens when I am confronted with inappropriate behavior. If it is something minor that turns out to be nothing more than a child

Perceptions

soliciting attention, I usually ignore it and try to immediately find something positive to bring to their attention. For anything on a larger scale of severity, I usually move the child from the group, but never from the classroom. A child in the hallway or principal's office misses instruction and does not have the opportunity to observe all of the fun they could have had. There are a few so-called "acceptable" disciplinary methods that I choose not to use. I paddle canoes and Ping-Pong balls, but never children. I move children, but never remove them. I do not make fun of children; I make fun for children. I do not yell at children in the classroom; I yell with them on the playground. I try not to ever refer to the classroom as being "mine." I assure the students that the proper substitution for the word "mine" should always be "ours."

MY STUDENTS . . .
THE TEACHERS

Just as a grandmother speaks of her grandchildren, it is important for me to speak of my children, the students. Actually, if I discussed all of the wonderful details concerning each and every student, I would end up writing another book, perhaps a novel, or maybe even a complete set of encyclopedias. Therefore, I decided to attempt the impossible task of selecting some of the more impressive children, doubly unique in character and stature.

First, I should put things into perspective. I have helped with the natural childbirth process of all three of my children. I was totally enthralled as I cut the umbilical cord of my first-born. With each child came the overwhelming emotions that can only be felt by observing life as it enters our world. I have expressed my feelings on numerous occasions to friends and relatives, and yet, regardless of how descriptively articulate I am, the consuming power of my emotions belittles the inadequacy of my words. I suppose an analogy could be found in the description of a gourmet meal. Regardless of how vivid the detailed description becomes, only the actual taste of each savory morsel can convey the true meaning of the experience. Therefore, no matter how I illustrate my daily experiences with my students, I realize that my words alone cannot properly evoke the feelings and emotions I have felt. The one message I can definitely state is that all children are completely different, and all children can learn.

Now that the stage is set, it is time to introduce the cast of characters — the students who taught the teacher. I will undoubtedly discuss these students for the rest of my life, but I suppose as the teaching years pass by, I will be forced to refer to them as my "grandstudents."

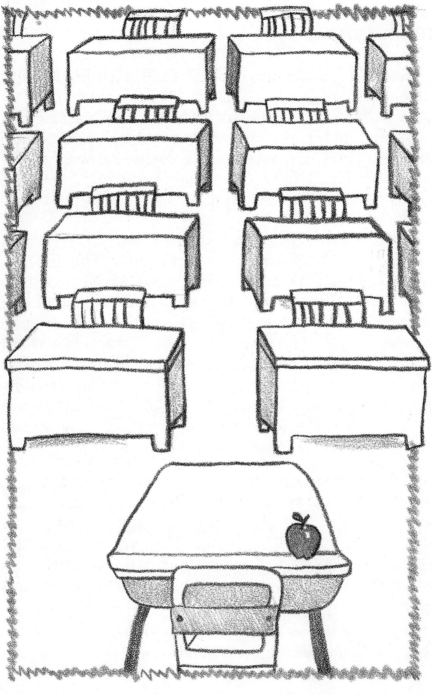

JUAN

While in the third trimester of her pregnancy, Juan's mother plummeted through the floor of a two-story building. There was extensive fetal damage and the baby ultimately had to be taken by cesarean. Living in a poverty stricken area of Puerto Rico, Mrs. Gonzales was subjected to astronomical medical bills. Juan was not fulfilling the doctors' expectations of a newborn, and it was determined that he would probably not make it through the night. He had been born with a severe neuromuscular disorder.

Juan spent the first five years of his life under the scientific security blanket of the hospital, and it was not until shortly after his fifth birthday that he was first released to go home. He had overcome the damaging effects of cerebral palsy as an infant and was confronted with the new challenges of daily physical therapy. He and his mother shared a one-room apartment above a small family-run grocery store. The people in the store aided him in developing social skills and provided him with free physical therapy. Each day, as his mother left for work, she would place Juan on a blanket in a specified aisle of the store. Throughout the day, the owner and his customers would roll cans of vegetables to him, expecting the cans to be rolled back or placed on a shelf. Although somewhat primitive, these initial physical therapy sessions proved to be a very encouraging sign for a boy who was "not expected to make it through the night." As his motor skills and hand-eye coordination began to improve, Juan's mother was told that Juan would never walk and that she should be proud of the accomplishments he had already made. This diagnosis, coupled with her undying faith, eventually led to their move to Houston.

Juan took his first steps as a seven-year-old. His dream was to return to the hospital of his youth and walk through the office doors of his pessimistic doctors. His speech was slurred, but quite intelligible. He had difficulty standing straight and displayed a scissored pattern in his walk. His left hand hooked inward and was subjected to continuous involuntary movement. Even as he slept, his hand remained plagued by motion.

Juan was placed in my classroom with the understanding that he was to sit at a full-sized table. He was to do all written work on a special typewriter with enlarged keys and a finger guard, and an aide was to be assigned to unfasten and fasten his trousers while in the restroom. Also, the aide was to be available at lunchtime to carry his lunch tray. After much conversation, deliberation, and tears, I convinced Mrs. Gonzales to trust my instincts as an educator and allow me the opportunity to teach Juan as close to the norm as possible. The philosophy behind my approach with Juan was simple: Those who believe they can do anything are probably right, but so are those who believe they can't.

When he entered my classroom, Juan was wearing a puzzled mask of dismay as he searched for his large table and sophisticated typewriter. In their absence, he found a student desk much like any other in the room. Eagerly resting on the top of this desk was an over-sized pencil, which was about as big around as two of his fingers taped together.

"Is there some mistake?" he asked hesitantly.

"Yes, there may very well be Juan," I began, "but we can often learn from our mistakes, can't we?"

His confusion took him by the hand and led him to his seat. I had placed pillows next to his desk. Due to his difficulty with balance, I thought there may be a chance he could tip out of his desk. By the end of the day, he had fallen out approximately eight times. When he had asked to use the restroom, he was shocked to hear that he did not have an aide. He went through three changes of clothing that day. His frustration mounted as he could not grip the pencil I gave him. At lunch he even had to carry his own tray which led to his accidentally dropping it on the floor, spewing its contents everywhere. I assured him that I would get him a second tray while he cleaned the results of the first. The most difficult aspect of that first day came in trying to avoid the sympathetic gestures of the students and teachers that passed Juan during his struggles. As a result, by the end of the day, I was not a very popular person.

Most of the first week remained unchanged. I retained the role of the cruel slave master getting my jollies out of beating up on the kid with cerebral palsy, as opposed to the patient, caring, sympathetic teacher I was expected to be. When Juan confronted my tactics, I explained to him that, contrary to what the doctors had told him, he was definitely not handicapped. He could do everything anyone else could do. His strategy may be different, but the results would always be the same. A handicap was an attitude and not an ailment. When people think they cannot do as others, they are indeed handicapped. When those same people apply for a job someday, they will not be handed a specialized typewriter with a finger guard to fill out the application. I felt I gave him sound advice. He reciprocated with a silent stare.

As time passed, Juan improved tremendously. It was rare to see him fall from his desk, and I removed the pillows. It was rare to see him wet himself, and I sent his extra clothing home. It was rare to see him drop his lunch tray, and he spent his entire lunch period eating instead of cleaning. As he began to put his physical struggles behind him, he noticed his academic potential in front of him. His handwriting became legible, and his self-confidence dominated his capabilities. I marveled at his personality when he would make spontaneous statements such as, "If other students laugh at the way I walk, then they are the ones who are handicapped. Worse than that, I was born the way I am, but they chose to be handicapped!" I always had a personal respect and appreciation for Juan's perception of things. While racing the other children, he would fall and immediately get up and finish the race, usually long after the other children had gone on to another activity. I always made it a point to be at the finish line with a checkered flag pat on the back. He had a knack of making last place far more prestigious than first.

Eventually, I mainstreamed Juan out of my special education class and into the regular classes – one subject at a time – until he seemed to be out of my room more than he was in it. Before completely digesting elementary school, Juan was honored as "Safety Patrol of the Year." He also received the "Outstanding Student Progress Award." As an excess of six hundred children and parents applauded his achievements, he interrupted them by asking me to join him on stage. Now curious with silence, the audience listened as he told them, "Mr. 'G' took my table and gave me a desk. He took my typewriter and gave me a pencil. He gave me responsibility by putting a lunch tray in my hands and a safety belt across my shoulder. If it were not for all of my teachers, I would not be here today." My eyes swelled with pride.

I do not worry about Juan. He fought his way out of the hospital and into the aisles of the grocery store; he defied the odds by climbing to the top of the world. I have a feeling he will always be there. I think he even took me part of the way with him. I spend the better part of my teaching challenging students. I found it gratifying to have that challenge returned.

Juan's presence remains a challenge for all. He took his zest for life and combined it with his mother's passion for promise. That is how I will remember him.

TODD

Todd is an extremely likable child who manifests the qualities of a leader. In other words, Todd has been diagnosed with what I like to call the "Eddie Haskell Syndrome." On any given day, I may be standing at my classroom door greeting the children as they shuffle in to begin their day. Sensing his presence, I am promptly greeted with a strong, articulate, "Good morning Mr. 'G' ... and what a delightful pair of slacks you're wearing today," which he would follow with a spectacular grin. "And my, my – that shirt sure is a wonderful complement to those slacks!" he would add. "Good morning Todd. Thank you Todd. Come on in Todd." Todd would capture the attention of his classmates with the declaration, "What a fantastic day we're going to have here with good ol' Mr. 'G,' huh?" At that point, he would spin around and offer, "May I sharpen every pencil on your desk?" Within two minutes of his offer, I would be confronted by three students claiming to be stabbing victims of a freshly sharpened pencil. True to most reruns, there seems to be no known cure for the Eddie Haskell Syndrome. In fact, Todd just may have a future as a shoe salesman.

JENNIFER

In the eyes of my male students, Jennifer was a goddess. She did not walk, she floated. She did not run, she soared gracefully. Her hair had a silky sheen that seemed to cascade through the air in slow motion. Her large, brown eyes sparkled with a gleam of friendliness that made her radiant. As her smile lifted her tender cheeks upward, she would exhibit an expression of warmth and compassion. Her presence was soothing, and her voice was soft and gentle. She dressed with the sophisticated elegance that could only be compared to that of a foreign model.

In actuality, Jennifer was no different than any of the other third-grade girls. She hated the boys. Her feet were always securely on the ground as she walked and ran. Her hair was usually tangled from the combination of wind and play. At the slightest mention of a boy, Jennifer would squint her brown eyes with anger, as her cheeks pushed the corners of her mouth down into a frown. Her presence was intimidating, and she screamed at the boys in the standard high shrill. She wore her favorite T-shirt every other day. She was a sweet student who always tried hard in class, but she was a typical third-grade female. The boys learned from Jennifer much of the same lesson I learned while in my third-grade coatroom from Tammy Thomas: love is blind. As for Jennifer, I believe her arm was always cocked and ready to strike out in retaliation to a classmate's first kiss.

BENJAMIN

Benjamin is an incredible young man. I use the term "young man" in the literal sense. He was the only eight-year-old boy I ever taught who had a mustache. He had a low voice that bellowed with honesty. His personality lent itself to that of an elderly man, complete with a receding hairline and a taunt round belly that relaxed over the edge of his belt, which usually refused to do its job. Benjamin seemed to cry frequently, which I always attributed to his overwhelming degree of honesty. I appreciated the fact that he was honest with himself and therefore depended on his emotions more than most children of the same age. Perhaps he will be able to channel those emotions into a career in community service someday.

One day, while doing various activities designed to strengthen visual awareness and short term memory, I asked Benjamin to observe a rose which had grown in the courtyard area of the school grounds. After a few minutes, we returned to the classroom, at which time I gave him a sheet of paper and asked him to draw and color everything he saw in a detailed reproduction. After approximately five minutes, Benjamin approached me with his picture announcing that he had finished. It was a wonderful picture of the rose, but he had left the remainder of the paper blank.

"Benjamin," I began, "this is a fantastic drawing so far. I can't wait to see it when it's finished."

"Oh, it is finished, Mr. 'G'," he quickly replied.

"No, I don't think you understand, Benjamin," I continued. "I would like for you to put everything that was actually out there in that courtyard beyond your rose into your picture."

"Well, that's all there was," he interrupted.

"Surely you remember all of those other objects making up the background for your colorful rose. I would like for you to include them as well," I pleaded.

"Well, that's all there was," he repeated.

"Okay, that's fine, Benjamin. Go ahead and title your picture and we will put it up on our bulletin board," I concluded. He labeled his picture "Sun Glooms." When I asked him if there was any particular reason he chose the title, he simply shrugged his shoulders with a nonchalant, "Not really." It became crystal clear why he chose that title once we went back out to view the courtyard. The courtyard was decorated with tall pine trees that used the afternoon sun to cast long, gloomy shadows around Benjamin's rose. I realized that Benjamin's mind had a cache of creative and perceptive images, but it was up to me to devise a way to get them out.

DERRICK AND TAYLOR

Being brothers, Derrick and Taylor had many similarities, but they were also very different. They were residents of the Coke Street Apartments. Although both boys had some learning disabilities, they had a street knowledge that was more valuable, at that point in their lives, than a college education. They were not afraid of the dark – they sometimes lived in it. They knew how to scale a barbed-wire fence without getting scratched. They knew how to convert a rusty nail affixed to a discarded broomstick into a tool that could spear frogs in the bayou, or free pecans from the stubborn branches of a pecan tree. They had devised strategies to trick the "park people" into spilling their dependency from its plain brown wrapper. They knew how to stalk field mice with the same finesse and courage as big game hunters. Their imaginations were colorfully vivid, and I was always intrigued by the descriptive stories of their daily adventures. It did not matter whether or not their tales were valid; they were selections from their indestructible, imaginative thoughts.

Before transferring to Kolter Elementary, I took the boys to a Theater Under the Stars production of *Scrooge*. We also devoted an entire Saturday together exploring the mystical world of an astronaut at the Johnson Space Center/NASA. I guess I felt the excursions would add an exciting twist to some of their experiences and therefore allow me the honor of contributing to their golden imaginations.

Incidentally, I remember Derrick and Taylor as being two of the children gripping the chain link fence while peering at me with questioning eyes. Also, it was Derrick who enlightened my first teaching assignment with the memorable, straight-faced contribution, "Green, green, yo' bootie ain't clean."

MELINDA

Melinda either had an extremely slick nose, or her glasses were slightly too large. She spent a great deal of time bypassing the lenses and peering over the top edge. I always thought it was interesting how she would never forget to wear them, but always forgot to use them. She had curly, black hair, which she used more as a head cover than a fashion statement. She was tall and very personable. Melinda's story is one which is permanently engraved in the "fondness" chapter of my book of memories.

I instructed Melinda to draw and color her absolute favorite playground activity. Due to her love for the ball-bouncing, four-squared, blacktop game, she immediately began her picture. The actual game is played on a blacktop outlined with yellow paint highlighting the numbers "one," "four," "two," and "three." Much to my surprise, Melinda's finished project portrayed a yellow top outlined with black paint highlighting the numbers "four," "one," "three," and "two." Her picture depicted an exact mirror reversal in every detail. Naturally, this discovery literally grabbed my eyebrows and shot them straight up, causing an instant wrinkle of confusion on my forehead — which I immediately began rubbing. Melinda was not dyslexic, nor had she ever displayed any signs of a reversal problem. Pointing to the lower case alphabet above the blackboard, I quickly asked Melinda to name the letters "b," "d," "p," and "q," which are letters commonly reversed. I then asked her to write them on a piece of paper. Both of my impromptu evaluations uncovered absolutely nothing, as she very confidently responded with the appropriate answers. I then asked Melinda to turn her back on the alphabet. I showed her flash cards of the same letters out of sequence. Her attempts were both negative and positive: negative in that she responded in error each time, and positive in that I had begun to unravel her compensatory scheme. I observed her closely as she rewrote the letters. In making the letter "b," she drew a straight line, came over to the "d" side of the line, drew an imaginary circle, and completed the letter on the opposite side. She had defined and refined the classic art of compensation. This chameleon effect both fooled me into thinking that she did not have a reversal problem and at the same time, taught me she did. People who are color blind identify a color incorrectly only once. They then compensate by asking someone to reveal the actual color. From that point on, every time they see the incorrect color, they identify it as the actual color.

With the satisfaction of winning the war came the feelings of pride in watching Melinda progress. Whether she looked through her glasses or over them, her progress was partly in the hands of my instructional modifications. Melinda challenged me, quite by accident. I accepted her challenge and together we both learned a great deal.

BONNIE

Bonnie is one of the cutest children in the world. A very petite girl, she had blond hair and blue eyes. She was a smart child, but I couldn't take my eyes off of her for more than thirty seconds at a time. During the only year I had her in my class, she ate paste, gave herself a haircut, sucked the ink out of her pen, colored her teeth with crayons, erased the skin off her arm, scribbled on her new shoes with a permanent marker, ate my Valentine's Day candy, erased my boardwork, shoved miniature wads of paper up her nostrils, glued her pencils to the inside of her supply box, fed flecks of glitter to the fish, removed the "a" key from the computer keyboard, converted her desktop into an abstract painting, collected pencil shavings, and returned from lunch every day resembling a walking menu. Although parent conferences were somewhat awkward, she will always be one of my favorite students.

STEPHANIE

Stephanie is a child who "planted beans in kiddygarden," had a "spinach teacher" teach her a foreign language, and got a "science headache" from the high pollen count. She had a profound expression for words, which lacked in accuracy, but sparkled with creativity. When I first met Stephanie, she had developed an appetite for inappropriate behavior and therefore had many feathers in her cap, most of which she had plucked from an undisciplined blue jay. Her appetite for discipline eventually disrupted her hunger for learning and reserved her a table in my restaurant – the generic classroom.

It is much easier to pet a harmless kitten than a ferocious lion. Stephanie was not used to the occasional hugs of approval. She was large for her age and had a very intimidating physical presence. Her classmates always felt her presence in the classroom, often in the form of a scratch or a bruise. She had a 75% hearing loss in one ear and a very loud voice. I realized that Stephanie did exactly what people expected her to do. She was mean to the other students and unfortunately to herself as well. Perhaps she completely forgot what it was like to shine. I knew what needed to be done. After all, no matter how difficult it is, or how long it takes to clean, there is nothing more beautiful than polished sterling. I also knew that with a little attention and preventive maintenance, sterling would never tarnish again.

Stephanie grew to despise me. She hated school because I was her teacher. She would yell when I hugged her, frown when I smiled at her, and cry when I refused to back down to her stubbornness. After several days of anger, Stephanie chose to explore what she had been missing. One day she even went as far as to enjoy herself during a lesson and blush when

I hugged her. As she began to lift the downward crease of her eyebrows, I saw a change in her. I found a soft teddy bear trapped inside of a grizzly. As each day passed, the grizzly came to school less and less, therefore creating a vacant seat on the school bus for the teddy bear. It would not be accurate to say that the grizzly hibernated, but it did stay in its angry cave much more than it used to. As a result, Stephanie started learning to learn all over again. It was indeed a gratifying experience for everyone – especially me.

JONATHAN

I had heard so many negative things concerning Jonathan prior to his enrollment that I chose not to review his records when they arrived. Sometimes records turn out to be nothing more than a collection of teachers who never learned from the child, as opposed to the other way around. I did choose, however, to read his medical and family background.

Jonathan was born in 1980 in Houston. Although his grandmother and great aunt were thrilled with his arrival, his mother was young and single. She had many dreams, none of which included a newborn child. After a few short days of anger and dispute, Jonathan's mother vanished to the West coast, and his life became a product of his grandmother and great aunt's love and caring.

Living on welfare, Jonathan found the pleasures of life were simple; people were as happy as they allowed themselves to be. Therefore, Jonathan was happy and had a group of friends who shared his happiness. Jonathan treasured the warmth and acceptance of his two mothers and felt secure with their loving guidance. Within four days of his eighth birthday, both Jonathan's grandmother and great aunt died unexpectedly of natural causes. Without having an adequate period of time to grieve his losses, Jonathan was introduced to his mother for the first time in his life. In her absence, she had married a man with four children and given birth to four of her own. Due to the circumstances, the family chose to reside in Houston. They basically said, "Jonathan, I am your mother, this is your stepfather, and these are your eight brothers and sisters. We have arranged for you to be bused to another school beginning tomorrow."

One school year passed. During this year, Jonathan had four teachers, no friends, and a label, which was a gift from the school system. His label, "emotionally disturbed," qualified him for the program I was teaching at the time. Since his school did not house such a program, he was bused to my school and enrolled. This was the information I had on Jonathan the first time we met.

I decided that I did not know Jonathan. I knew of Jonathan, but did not know him. This was the approach I took concerning my initial impressions of him. He had a deep, gruff voice, which he chose not to use much. His appearance was unkempt, which did not seem to bother him much, nor did it bother me. He assumed sort of a robotic position consisting of, "I'm here. I have to be here. Tell me what to do." He was extremely withdrawn – no classroom participation or social interaction. I could not reach Jonathan.

The day was Wednesday. I thought it might be fun to do some visual awareness activities from the *Polaroid Education Program Lesson/Activity Book*. Using a Polaroid Instant Camera, the students were to select something to photograph. Before they could see the developed photograph, they had to first draw it in vivid detail, color it, and give it a title. Little did

I know that this would be an activity designed to teach the teacher.

Once handed the camera, Jonathan burst through the classroom door with a determination I had never seen in him. It was my quick-paced curiosity that kept me up with his motivational strides. He took the most direct route available to the bicycle rack. To me, the bicycle rack was nothing more than a fenced rectangular section of pavement used to secure the personal property of students during the school day. Over the next few days I found my description to be completely inadequate. It was definitely far more than I ever perceived it to be.

As his enthusiasm collided with his excitement, Jonathan took a photograph of the bicycle rack from the outside looking through the fence. Without saying a word, I reached in front of Jonathan and stimulated his curiosity by removing his photograph and walking in the direction of the classroom. He had a tremendous urge to see his photograph. It was a product of his success, and he began to relish the anticipated outcome of the instant developing process. After what seemed to be an eternity to Jonathan, we finally arrived at the classroom. I quickly interrupted his persistent pleading by explaining he must first draw and color the anticipated product of his photography excursion.

He drew a wonderful picture with colorful, imaginative simplicity. The fence was yellow and very bold. Behind it were two objects resembling bicycles. One was blue and the other red. He felt he had finished and asked to see his photograph. Jonathan did not say anything with his voice as he gazed at his new experience, but his eyes had lots of fantastic things to say. I was very pleased with the effect of the activity, and I asked him to title his picture. Without thought, Jonathan wrote the words "Friends' Gate" in quick letters across the bottom of his drawing. I must confess, I was really taken by the peculiarity of his title and was more than anxious to discover its roots.

"Your photograph turned out perfect, Jonathan!" I began. "Your picture is every bit as nice, but I'm really excited about your title. Would you tell me something about it?" His response was a mere shrug of his shoulders. "Now wait a second, Jonathan," I said. "You came up with a fabulous title without even taking the time to think it over. What does 'Friends' Gate' mean to you? I mean, why not 'Bike Rack' or 'Jonathan's Picture'? Why 'Friends' Gate'?" I became discouraged with the second shrug of his shoulders as I knew the interpretation of his title was securely with Jonathan and the property of his imagination.

As the days passed, "Friends' Gate" became my personal obsession. Who would have thought that Jonathan's imagination and my obsession would join forces in the ongoing effort to reach and teach Jonathan.

It was Monday morning and I began making my routine safety rounds of the school. I was assigned the duty of being the supervisor of the Safety Patrol Program. On that particular morning, I was greeted by two over-excited patrols who were upset with the "new kid" in my class. It seems that Jonathan was not complying with the school rule of retreating to the playground after getting off the bus. He had strategically placed himself at the front corner of the building where he had been staring at the bicycle rack on a daily basis. I decided to encourage the patrols to ignore the entire situation, and I assured them that I would personally deal with it. I felt the best approach would be for me to find my corner of the building and stare at the bicycle rack for a few days so I could assess Jonathan's fascination. After two days I understood. My obsession had overcome Jonathan's secret of "Friends' Gate." The bicycle rack clique was unique to only those who ride their bicycles to school each day. In comparison, this is equivalent to high school students who are lucky enough to drive their own cars to school. I witnessed the same group of children each day as they proudly strolled their two-wheeled vehicles through the metal gate, which was their door to friendship. Once inside the gate, the students would assume a casual slouch against the fence, or perhaps sit side-saddle on their bicycle seats, and engage in action-packed conversations with one another. The only students allowed inside the bicycle rack were those who rode bicycles to school. This, of course, added to the mystic aura of the clique. Eventually, the school bells would call out to the students, and the casual swing of the backpacks would begin toward the building as the gate clinked shut.

It seemed clear to me what the next move needed to be. That evening I led a successful expedition in search of an old, used bicycle from a garage sale. The following morning I pointed out the carelessness of a student who had left his bicycle at the side of the building. I asked Jonathan to assume the responsibility of making sure the wandering bicycle found its proper place in the bicycle rack. This particular bicycle, however, had the annoying, recurring habit of showing up each morning, and I had to enlist Jonathan's assistance each day. After three days there was a new face casually exchanging conversation with the clique. Although Jonathan eventually uncovered my scheme, it seemed practical for him to become the newly appointed, supervising safety patrol of the Kolter bicycle rack. I am pleased to report that Jonathan brought his new attitude into the classroom, which included participating and socializing. He even began doing normal things, such as poking kids in line and throwing an occasional crust of bread across the cafeteria.

To Jonathan, the gate of the bicycle rack meant friendship. Beyond this gate was a feeling of belonging. Being a part of a circle of friends meant first passing through "Friends' Gate." I like to think that Jonathan's gate was my cigar box. Although it was the same to everyone else, this gate was much different to Jonathan: it was his.

Two months later, Jonathan's family relocated and I never saw him again. I will never forget my experiences with Jonathan. He had the creative ability to allow his imagination to merge with his insight and feelings. I took the opportunity to learn from Jonathan, and I thanked him for that. I can only hope to be as good a teacher as Jonathan was.

EPILOGUE

Last summer I went back to Jefferson Elementary School, the building that breathed. Although the building had not functioned as a school for several years, it still seemed to have its inhaling qualities. The floors were every bit as shiny as they were in 1963. The brick ·pillars, the suspended lights, the blacktop – all were left unchanged. I was able to travel back to a time when my biggest fear was leaving my mother's side and my biggest joy was the priceless contents of my supply box. I felt like I had gone home after being away much too long. I was suddenly thirsty for an ice-cold bottle of milk – with a paper straw of course. Slipping my hands in my pockets, I shuffled to the rear of the building and peered through the windows of my kindergarten classroom. Then I heard the most horrifying scream. It came from a large gray flying saucer mounted on the wall. I immediately felt as if I needed to be somewhere. Since the building was locked, I left. On my way back to the car, I took a shortcut through the playground. Standing amongst the pebbles, I had wonderful images of past playground adventures.

As I slowly drove away, I glanced in the rear-view mirror of my imagination and smiled. There was Mrs. Towers, with broom in hand, keeping the blacktop a safe and pebble-free place for my childhood memories to run.